TOKYO DISNEYLAND TRAVEL AND ADVENTURE GUIDE 2025

Discover the Magic of TOKYO DISNEYLAND, Explore its Seven Themed Lands, New Attractions for 2025, Special Shows and Parades, Seasonal Events and Hidden Gems

ELENA S. LUIS

All rights reserved. No part of this publication may be reproduced, distributed, or transmitted in any form or by any means, including photocopying, recording, or other electronic or mechanical methods, without the prior written permission of the publisher, except in the case of brief quotations embodied in critical reviews and certain other noncommercial uses permitted by copyright law.

Copyright © Elena S. Luis, 2025.

Table of Contents

Introduction 8
    Why Visit Tokyo Disneyland in 2025 10
    What Makes Tokyo Disneyland Unique? 12
    Who Is This Guide For? 14

Practical Information 17
    Location and How to Get There 17
    Entry Requirements and Tickets 19
    Best Time to Visit 21
    Accessibility and Facilities 23

Accommodation Options 29
    On-Site Disney Hotels 29
    Nearby Hotels and Alternative Stays 32
    Budget vs. Luxury Stays 35

Park Overview 42
    History and Legacy of Tokyo Disneyland 42
    Themed Lands Overview 44
        World Bazaar 44
        Adventureland 45
        Westernland 46
        Critter Country 47
        Fantasyland 47
        Toontown 48
        Tomorrowland 49

Must-See Rides and Experiences 51
New Attractions for 2025 64
    "It's a Small World with Groot" 64
    Upcoming Wreck-It Ralph Attraction 66
Special Shows and Parades 70
Hidden Gems and Underrated Experiences 78
Cultural Insights 87
    Japanese Etiquette and Disney Magic 87
    Local Traditions Integrated into the Park 88
    Seasonal Events and Celebrations 90
Dining and Shopping 94
    Must-Try Foods and Snacks 94
    Themed Restaurants and Cafes 97
    Shopping for Souvenirs and Merchandise 99
    Seasonal Menus and Limited-Edition Items 101
Suggested Itineraries 103
    One-Day Adventure Plan 103
    Three-Day Immersive Experience 105
    Thematic Itineraries 107
        Family-Friendly Fun 107
        Thrill-Seeker's Guide 109
        Romantic Getaway 110
Transportation and Navigation 113
    Getting Around the Park 113
    Using the Disney Resort Line 114

Navigating Tokyo Disney Resort with Apps and Maps 116

Parking and Shuttle Services 117

Safety and Health Tips 119

Staying Safe in Crowded Areas 119

Preparing for Weather Changes 121

First Aid Stations and Emergency Services 122

COVID-19 Precautions and Updates 124

Packing and Preparation Tips 127

What to Pack for Your Disney Adventure 127

Essential Gear for Families with Kids 130

Recommended Apps and Tools 132

Insider Tips and Tricks 136

How to Avoid Long Lines 136

Best Times to Visit Popular Attractions 138

Where to Find the Best Photo Spots 139

Budget-Saving Hacks 141

Sustainability and Responsible Tourism 144

Eco-Friendly Practices at Tokyo Disneyland 144

How Visitors Can Support Sustainability 146

Respecting Local Culture and Environment 148

Resources and Contacts 152

Official Websites and Apps 152

Local Emergency Numbers 153

Conclusion 157

Final Tips for a Magical Adventure............................ 157

BONUS CHAPTER 161

Basic Greetings and Polite Expressions 161

Navigating the Park 162

At Restaurants and Cafes 163

Shopping for Souvenirs 164

Meeting Characters or Cast Members 165

Emergency Situations 166

Polite Small Talk 167

Miscellaneous Phrases 167

FAQs 170

General Information 170

Tickets and Reservations 171

Park Navigation 172

Attractions and Entertainment 173

Dining and Snacks 174

Families and Kids 175

Shopping and Souvenirs 176

Weather and Seasons 176

Health and Safety 177

Introduction

The moment I first stepped into Tokyo Disneyland, I felt a rush of emotions so powerful it was as if the child in me had woken up and taken over. The air shimmered with laughter, the scent of buttery popcorn drifted by, and Cinderella's Castle stood tall, a beacon of dreams and possibilities. It wasn't just a theme park it was a world of magic, wonder, and connection, unlike anything I had ever experienced. And trust me, after two decades of globetrotting, I've seen my fair share of extraordinary places.

But Tokyo Disneyland? It's something else. It's where Disney's timeless charm collides with Japan's unparalleled attention to detail and hospitality. Every moment feels intentional, every corner tells a story, and every guest is made to feel like the hero of their own fairy tale. As I write this, I can almost hear the familiar notes of the parade music drifting through the streets of World Bazaar, and I can picture the joy on a child's face as they meet their favorite Disney character for the very first time.

You're holding this guide because, like me, you crave more than just a vacation you're after an adventure. You want to know the secrets to unlocking the best of what Tokyo Disneyland has to offer, from the dazzling parades to the jaw-dropping new attractions planned for 2025. You want the inside scoop, the hidden gems, the tricks that will make your trip unforgettable. And I'm here to share it all with you.

This book is not just a collection of facts and figures; it's my personal journey woven into the essence of Tokyo Disneyland. I've walked these streets, waited in those lines, and laughed until my stomach hurt on those rides. I've found the coziest corners to enjoy a snack, the perfect time to catch the fireworks, and the best way to avoid feeling overwhelmed by the crowds. And now, I want you to feel as prepared and excited as I did every time I've stepped foot into this magical realm.

What makes Tokyo Disneyland in 2025 particularly special? Oh, where do I begin? Imagine the thrill of a brand-new ride that whisks you into the digital world of Wreck-It Ralph. Picture Groot, from Marvel's Guardians of the Galaxy, taking center stage in an enchanting twist on "It's a Small World." Feel the festive cheer of a holiday parade or the warm embrace of Japanese traditions woven into Disney's famous celebrations. This year promises to be a spectacle of innovation and nostalgia, and I can't wait for you to experience it.

But before we dive into the itineraries, dining tips, and insider hacks, I want you to do something. Close your eyes for a moment and picture yourself there. Hear the hum of excitement as families pour through the gates. Smell the sweetness of churros mingling with the fresh scent of popcorn. Feel the sun warming your face as you stand in front of Cinderella's Castle, your heart full of anticipation. That feeling? That's what this book is here to help you capture, plan for, and experience to the fullest.

This guide is more than a roadmap it's an invitation to dream, to connect, and to embrace the magic of Tokyo Disneyland in 2025. I'll be with you every step of the way, sharing everything I've learned so you can make memories that will last a lifetime. Adventure awaits, and trust me, you're about to embark on a journey that will leave you forever changed.

Are you ready? Let's dive in.

Why Visit Tokyo Disneyland in 2025

Imagine this: You've just passed through the gates of Tokyo Disneyland. The sound of cheerful music fills the air, and a burst of color and energy surrounds you. Families laugh, couples stroll hand-in-hand, and children's eyes light up as they spot their favorite Disney characters for the first time. Ahead of you stands Cinderella's Castle, gleaming in the sunlight, an iconic symbol of dreams coming true. Welcome to Tokyo Disneyland a place where magic doesn't just exist; it thrives.

But why is 2025 the perfect time to visit? Let me tell you it's a year like no other. Tokyo Disneyland is unveiling new attractions, hosting unforgettable seasonal celebrations, and continuing to blend Disney's classic charm with Japan's unmatched hospitality and innovation. Whether you're a seasoned Disney fan or it's your first trip, 2025 promises to be a landmark year, full of surprises and memories waiting to be made.

One of the most exciting additions this year is the all-new **Wreck-It Ralph attraction**, set in the heart of Tomorrowland. This highly anticipated ride invites you to dive into the digital universe alongside Ralph and Vanellope, offering cutting-edge technology and interactive elements that immerse you in the story. It's not just a ride it's an adventure that will leave you buzzing with excitement.

And then there's the limited-time overlay of **"It's a Small World with Groot"**. For the first half of 2025, Marvel fans will be delighted as Groot joins the classic attraction, bringing a fresh twist to this beloved favorite. It's the perfect blend of nostalgia and innovation, showcasing Tokyo Disneyland's ability to keep surprising its guests.

Beyond the rides, 2025 is brimming with special events. From the **New Year's celebration**, which fuses Japanese traditions with Disney magic, to the vibrant **summer festivals** and the enchanting **Halloween and Christmas parades**, every season offers something unique. Whether you're chasing cherry blossoms in the spring or basking in the glow of holiday lights in December, Tokyo Disneyland transforms itself with every turn of the calendar.

So, why visit Tokyo Disneyland in 2025? Because this is the year to embrace the extraordinary. It's a year where dreams are bigger, the magic is brighter, and the memories you'll make will be more unforgettable than ever.

What Makes Tokyo Disneyland Unique?

You might be wondering: What sets Tokyo Disneyland apart from other Disney parks around the world? After all, Disney magic exists in Florida,

California, Paris, and beyond. Let me tell you Tokyo Disneyland is in a league of its own.

First, there's the **Japanese attention to detail**. From the perfectly manicured gardens to the impeccably clean walkways, every inch of the park feels like it's been sprinkled with pixie dust. Cast Members (Disney's term for employees) go above and beyond to ensure your experience is nothing short of magical. Whether they're guiding you to an attraction, posing for a photo, or simply greeting you with a warm smile, their hospitality is second to none.

And then there's the **fusion of Disney and Japanese culture**. Nowhere else in the world will you find Mickey Mouse celebrating Japanese festivals or enjoying traditional mochi snacks. The park seamlessly blends Disney's global appeal with Japan's rich heritage, offering experiences you simply can't find anywhere else. The seasonal events, like **Tanabata Days** (a Japanese star festival celebrated with Disney characters in yukatas), bring the best of both worlds together.

The food at Tokyo Disneyland is another highlight. Picture this: You're biting into a fluffy Mickey-shaped churro or sipping on a seasonal, Instagram-worthy drink. Maybe you're enjoying a bowl of ramen at a themed restaurant or treating yourself to a limited-edition popcorn flavor matcha, caramel, or soy sauce butter. Dining here isn't just about fueling your energy; it's a culinary adventure in itself.

But perhaps what truly makes Tokyo Disneyland unique is its **ability to make every visitor feel special**. The park is designed with everyone in mind, from wide-eyed children experiencing the magic for the first time to thrill-seekers looking for adrenaline-pumping rides, and even nostalgic adults longing for a touch of childhood wonder.

And let's not forget about its sister park, **Tokyo Disney Sea**, located just next door. While Tokyo Disneyland is all about classic Disney charm, Disney Sea offers a completely different vibe with its ocean-inspired themes and more grown-up attractions. Together, they create a one-of-a-kind destination that appeals to every type of traveler.

If you've been to other Disney parks before, you'll notice the differences immediately. Tokyo Disneyland isn't just a park; it's an experience a perfect blend of storytelling, culture, and unparalleled magic.

Who Is This Guide For?

Now, you might be wondering if this guide is right for you. Let me ask you a question: Are you someone who dreams of a place where fantasy becomes reality, where every corner offers something new to discover, and where you can leave the stress of the world behind? If the answer is yes, then this guide is for you.

- **Families with Kids**: There's nothing quite like seeing a child's face light up as they meet their favorite Disney character or take their first ride on Dumbo the Flying Elephant. This guide is packed with tips to make your family trip smooth and magical, from navigating strollers to finding the best kid-friendly attractions.

- **Couples and Honeymooners**: Tokyo Disneyland is also a destination for romance. Imagine watching the nighttime fireworks hand-in-hand or sharing a quiet moment on the Mark Twain Riverboat. This guide will help you craft a romantic itinerary filled with unforgettable moments.

- **Solo Travelers**: Think Tokyo Disneyland is only for groups? Think again! There's something incredibly liberating about exploring the park solo. You can take your time, ride your favorite attractions multiple times, and enjoy the freedom to do exactly what you want.

- **Disney Fans**: Whether you've visited every Disney park around the world or you're a lifelong fan finally making the pilgrimage to Tokyo Disneyland, this guide will help you discover the unique features that make this park a must-see.

- **Adventure Seekers**: For those who crave a bit more thrill in their Disney experience, Tokyo Disneyland delivers. From the high-speed loops of Space Mountain to the water-filled excitement of Splash Mountain, this guide will show you how to make the most of every adrenaline-pumping moment.

- **Foodies**: If your travel plans revolve around what to eat, this guide will not disappoint. We'll take you on a culinary tour of the park, highlighting the must-try snacks, unique dishes, and limited-edition treats you won't find anywhere else.

No matter who you are or where you come from, this guide is designed to make your visit as magical, seamless, and memorable as possible. It's written with you in mind, combining practical tips, insider secrets, and personal stories to help you create a trip that's perfectly tailored to you.

Practical Information

Planning a trip to Tokyo Disneyland is an exciting endeavor, and having the right information can make your experience seamless and enjoyable. Let's explore the essential details to ensure you're well-prepared for your magical journey.

Location and How to Get There

Location: Tokyo Disneyland is situated in Urayasu, Chiba Prefecture, just east of Tokyo. It's part of the Tokyo Disney Resort, which also includes Tokyo DisneySea.

Address: 1-1 Maihama, Urayasu, Chiba 279-0031, Japan

Getting There:

- **By Train:**
    - **From Tokyo Station:**
        - **JR Keiyo Line or JR Musashino Line:** Board a train bound for Maihama Station. The journey takes approximately 15 minutes and costs around ¥220. Maihama Station is

adjacent to the park entrance, making it a convenient option.

- **From Narita Airport:**
    - **Narita Express & JR Lines:** Take the Narita Express to Tokyo Station (about 60 minutes), then transfer to the JR Keiyo Line to Maihama Station (15 minutes). The total journey is around 75 minutes. If you have a Japan Rail Pass, this route is fully covered.

- **From Haneda Airport:**
    - **Tokyo Monorail & JR Lines:** Ride the Tokyo Monorail to Hamamatsucho Station (13 minutes), transfer to the JR Yamanote Line to Tokyo Station (6 minutes), and then take the JR Keiyo Line to Maihama Station (15 minutes). The entire trip takes approximately 45 minutes.

- **By Bus:**
    - **Airport Limousine Bus:** Direct buses operate from both Narita and Haneda Airports to Tokyo Disneyland. From Narita, the journey is about 75 minutes and costs ¥1,800

for adults and ¥900 for children. From Haneda, it's approximately 50 minutes, with fares around ¥1,000 for adults and ¥500 for children.

- **By Car:**
    - **Parking:** For those driving, parking is available at Tokyo Disneyland. Fees are ¥2,500 on weekdays and ¥3,000 on weekends and holidays.

Quick Tips:

- **IC Cards:** Utilize rechargeable IC cards like Suica or Pasmo for convenient travel on trains and buses.
- **Early Arrival:** Aim to arrive early, especially during peak seasons, to make the most of your day.

Entry Requirements and Tickets

Entry Requirements:

- **Visa:** Ensure your passport is valid for the duration of your stay. Depending on your nationality, a visa may be required to enter Japan. It's advisable to check the latest visa requirements before your trip.

Tickets:

- **1-Day Passport:**
    - **Price:** Starting at approximately $57 USD (¥6,500), varying by season and age group.
    - **Includes:** Full-day admission to Tokyo Disneyland.

- **2-Day Passport:**
    - **Price:** Starting at around $114 USD (¥13,000), with variations based on season and age.
    - **Includes:** Admission to Tokyo Disneyland and/or Tokyo DisneySea over two consecutive days.

- **Purchasing Options:**
    - **Official Website:** Tickets can be purchased directly through the Tokyo Disney Resort official website.
    - **Authorized Resellers:** Platforms like Klook offer tickets with instant access via mobile QR codes, allowing you to skip the ticket lines.

Quick Tips:

- **Advance Purchase:** Buy tickets in advance to secure your preferred dates, especially during peak seasons.
- **Children's Admission:** Children under 4 years old enjoy free admission.

Best Time to Visit

Choosing the optimal time to visit can enhance your experience, balancing pleasant weather and manageable crowd levels.

Seasons:

- **Spring (March to May):**
    - **Pros:** Mild temperatures and the beauty of cherry blossoms.
    - **Cons:** Late March to early April can be crowded due to spring break and cherry blossom viewing.
- **Summer (June to August):**
    - **Pros:** Extended Park hours and vibrant summer events.
    - **Cons:** High temperatures, humidity, and potential typhoons.
- **Autumn (September to November):**

- **Pros:** Comfortable weather and stunning fall foliage.
    - **Cons:** Early September may experience residual summer heat.
- **Winter (December to February):**
    - **Pros:** Festive holiday decorations and lower crowd levels.
    - **Cons:** Cold temperatures; some attractions may close for maintenance.

Peak Periods to Avoid:

- **Golden Week:** Late April to early May; a series of national holidays leading to increased attendance.
- **Obon Festival:** Mid-August; a traditional holiday period with higher travel activity.
- **New Year's Holidays:** Late December to early January; a popular time for both locals and tourists.

Quick Tips:

- **Weekdays vs. Weekends:** Visiting on weekdays typically results in shorter wait times compared to weekends.

- **Special Events:** Check the park's event calendar for seasonal celebrations that might interest you.

Accessibility and Facilities

Tokyo Disneyland is committed to providing an enjoyable experience for everyone, regardless of physical abilities or specific needs. From easy navigation to thoughtful facilities, the park ensures all guests can experience the magic seamlessly.

Accessibility Features:

- **Wheelchair Access:**
    - Most attractions, restaurants, and facilities are wheelchair accessible.
    - Wheelchairs can be rented at the park for ¥500 per day. Electric carts are also available for ¥2,000 per day, but they are limited in number, so early rental is recommended.
    - Special viewing areas for parades and shows are designated for guests using wheelchairs.
- **Accessible Restrooms:**
    - Wheelchair-accessible restrooms are available throughout the park. They

are clearly marked on the park map and include spacious interiors for ease of use.

- **Attraction Accommodations:**
    - Many attractions have accessibility-friendly entrances or modified boarding processes. Check with Cast Members at each ride for specific instructions.

- **Hearing and Visual Assistance:**
    - The park provides Braille maps for visually impaired guests.
    - Guests with hearing impairments can request a Handheld Captioning device or written attraction scripts at Guest Relations.

Family-Friendly Amenities:

- **Baby Care Centers:**
    - Tokyo Disneyland features baby care centers equipped with nursing rooms, diaper-changing stations, and highchairs for feeding.
    - Locations: One near the entrance of World Bazaar and another in Toontown.

- **Stroller Rentals:**
    - Strollers can be rented for ¥1,000 per day. These are especially helpful for families with young children to navigate the large park.
- **Kid-Specific Spaces:**
    - Toontown is an ideal area for younger visitors, offering interactive attractions, character meet-and-greets, and play areas designed for little ones.

Dietary Needs and Food Restrictions:

- **Allergen-Friendly Options:**
    - Many restaurants offer allergen-free meals upon request. Simply inform a Cast Member of your dietary needs, and they'll assist you in finding suitable options.
    - The official website and park app provide detailed allergen information for most menu items.
- **Vegetarian and Vegan Choices:**
    - While vegetarian and vegan options are somewhat limited, dishes like vegetable curry or pasta are available

in select restaurants. Ask for assistance at any dining location.

Technology for Convenience:

- **Tokyo Disney Resort App:**
    - Download the app before your visit to access a host of features, including attraction wait times, show schedules, and mobile food ordering.
    - The app also allows you to reserve attractions using the Disney Premier Access system, book dining reservations, and purchase merchandise online.

- **Free Wi-Fi:**
    - Complimentary Wi-Fi is available in most areas of the park, ensuring you stay connected throughout your visit.

Lockers and Storage:

- **Locker Rentals:**
    - Coin-operated lockers are located near the entrance of the park and at various key areas. Prices range from ¥300 to ¥700, depending on the size.

- These lockers are perfect for storing extra clothing, souvenirs, or heavy bags.

Service Animal Policy:

- Service animals are welcome in the park and on most attractions, provided they meet specific guidelines.
- Relief areas for service animals are clearly marked on the park map.

Medical Assistance:

- **First Aid Stations:**
  - Fully equipped First Aid Stations are located near World Bazaar. Trained medical staff are available to assist with minor injuries or health concerns.

- **Pharmacy Needs:**
  - While there isn't a pharmacy within the park, basic over-the-counter medications can be provided by First Aid staff. For more specialized needs, pharmacies are available near Maihama Station.

Quick Tips:

- **Early Planning:** If you require specific accommodations, contact Guest Relations ahead of time to ensure your needs are met.

- **Park Maps:** Grab an accessibility-friendly park map at the entrance or download one via the Tokyo Disney Resort app.

- **Rest Breaks:** Utilize shaded seating areas or quieter spots like Critter Country for breaks during busy hours.

With these facilities and features, Tokyo Disneyland ensures every visitor feels welcome and cared for. Whether you're a parent with young children, a guest with accessibility needs, or someone looking to make the most of modern conveniences, the park's thoughtful design and services make your experience magical from start to finish.

Accommodation Options

Planning where to stay during your Tokyo Disneyland adventure is crucial for a comfortable and memorable experience. Let's explore various accommodation options, from immersive on-site Disney hotels to convenient nearby alternatives, catering to diverse preferences and budgets.

On-Site Disney Hotels

Staying at an official Disney hotel offers unparalleled convenience and a touch of magic throughout your visit. Here are some top choices:

Tokyo Disneyland Hotel

- **Overview:** As the closest hotel to Tokyo Disneyland, this Victorian-inspired establishment immerses you in elegance and Disney charm.
- **Room Types and Rates:**
  - **Standard Rooms:** Starting at approximately ¥50,000 per night, accommodating up to four guests.

- o **Character Rooms:** Themed rooms featuring beloved Disney characters, starting around ¥70,000 per night.

- **Pros:**

    - o **Proximity:** Directly adjacent to the park entrance, allowing for easy access.

    - o **Themed Experience:** Intricate Disney-themed décor enhances the magical atmosphere.

    - o **Guest Benefits:** Early Park entry and exclusive merchandise opportunities.

- **Cons:**

    - o **Cost:** Higher price point compared to other accommodations.

    - o **Availability:** High demand requires booking well in advance.

Disney Ambassador Hotel

- **Overview:** This Art Deco-style hotel combines 1930s American glamour with Disney whimsy, located a short shuttle ride from the parks.

- **Room Types and Rates:**
  - **Standard Rooms:** Starting at approximately ¥45,000 per night.
  - **Character Rooms:** Featuring themes like Mickey Mouse and Donald Duck, starting around ¥65,000 per night.
- **Pros:**
  - **Themed Dining:** Home to Chef Mickey, where guests can dine with Disney characters.
  - **Guest Benefits:** Early Park entry and complimentary shuttle service.
- **Cons:**
  - **Distance:** Not within walking distance; relies on shuttle transport.
  - **Price:** Still on the higher end of the budget spectrum.

Tokyo Disney Celebration Hotel

- **Overview:** A more budget-friendly Disney hotel option, located approximately 15 minutes by shuttle from the parks, offering whimsical décor inspired by Disney attractions.

- **Room Types and Rates:**
    - **Standard Rooms:** Starting at approximately ¥30,000 per night.
    - **Family Rooms:** Accommodating larger groups, starting around ¥40,000 per night.
- **Pros:**
    - **Affordability:** More economical while still providing Disney-themed experiences.
    - **Guest Benefits:** Early Park entry and complimentary shuttle service.
- **Cons:**
    - **Distance:** Farther from the parks compared to other Disney hotels.
    - **Limited Amenities:** Fewer on-site dining and entertainment options.

Nearby Hotels and Alternative Stays

If on-site Disney hotels don't align with your preferences or budget, there are numerous nearby accommodations offering comfort and convenience.

Sheraton Grande Tokyo Bay Hotel

- **Overview:** A 4.5-star hotel located within the Tokyo Disney Resort area, offering spacious rooms and a variety of amenities.

- **Rates:** Rooms starting at approximately ¥25,000 per night.

- **Pros:**
    - **Proximity:** Close to the parks with easy monorail access.
    - **Amenities:** Multiple dining options, pools, and recreational facilities.

- **Cons:**
    - **Non-Disney Themed:** Lacks the immersive Disney décor of on-site hotels.
    - **Additional Costs:** Some amenities may incur extra charges.

Hotel Okura Tokyo Bay

- **Overview:** A luxury hotel offering elegant rooms and top-notch service, situated near the Disney Resort Line.

- **Rates:** Rooms starting at approximately ¥28,000 per night.

- **Pros:**
  - **Spacious Rooms:** Generously sized accommodations compared to typical Tokyo hotels.
  - **Dining:** Several on-site restaurants offering diverse cuisines.
- **Cons:**
  - **Distance:** Requires monorail or shuttle to reach the parks.
  - **Price:** Higher rates may not suit all budgets.

Tokyo Bay Maihama Hotel First Resort

- **Overview:** An official Tokyo Disney Resort hotel offering themed rooms and convenient access to the parks.
- **Rates:** Rooms starting at approximately ¥20,000 per night.
- **Pros:**
  - **Themed Rooms:** Options like "Frontier Room" provide a unique experience.
  - **Proximity:** Close to the parks with shuttle services available.

- **Cons:**
    - **Aging Facilities:** Some areas may feel dated compared to newer hotels.
    - **Crowds:** Being a popular choice, it can be busy, especially during peak seasons.

Alternative Accommodations:

- **Airbnb and Vacation Rentals:** For larger groups or longer stays, renting an apartment or house in the Urayasu area can offer more space and the comforts of home. Prices vary but can start as low as ¥10,000 per night.
- **Hostels and Guesthouses:** Budget travelers might consider hostels in nearby areas like Funabashi or Chiba, with dormitory beds starting around ¥3,000 per night.

Budget vs. Luxury Stays

Whether you're splurging on a dream vacation or keeping costs low, Tokyo Disneyland offers a range of accommodations to suit your budget and travel style. Here's a closer look at the options for both ends of the spectrum.

Luxury Stays

For travelers who want the full magical experience with all the perks, luxury accommodations provide a premium touch.

- **Tokyo Disneyland Hotel**:
    - **Why Choose This?** Staying here is like stepping into a Disney fairy tale. From elegant Victorian-inspired architecture to themed character rooms, this hotel offers an immersive experience that's hard to beat.
    - **Added Perks:** Guests get early park entry, priority booking for restaurants and shows, and an unbeatable location right next to the park gates.
    - **Budget Consideration:** Rates starting at ¥50,000 per night make it a premium choice, but the added convenience and magical ambiance often justify the cost.
- **Sheraton Grande Tokyo Bay Hotel**:
    - **Why Choose This?** A blend of luxury and convenience, this hotel is part of the Tokyo Disney Resort area and provides resort-style amenities

such as pools, a fitness center, and multiple dining options.

- **Added Perks:** Many rooms come with stunning views of Tokyo Bay or the park itself, making your stay feel even more special.

- **Budget Consideration:** Starting at approximately ¥25,000 per night, it's slightly more affordable than on-site Disney hotels, while still delivering a high-end experience.

- **Hotel Okura Tokyo Bay:**

  - **Why Choose This?** Known for its spacious rooms and exceptional service, this hotel combines Japanese elegance with modern luxury.

  - **Added Perks:** The hotel's restaurants serve exquisite cuisine, and its proximity to the Disney Resort Line makes transportation easy.

  - **Budget Consideration:** Rates starting at ¥28,000 per night make it a worthwhile splurge for comfort and style.

Mid-Range Options

Travelers looking for comfort without breaking the bank will find plenty of mid-range accommodations with excellent amenities.

- **Tokyo Disney Celebration Hotel**:
    - **Why Choose This?** This is the most affordable of the Disney hotels, yet it still offers themed décor and access to the magic.
    - **Added Perks:** Complimentary shuttle services to the park and early entry privileges make it a great choice for families on a budget.
    - **Budget Consideration:** Rooms start at ¥30,000 per night, offering good value for the Disney experience.
- **Tokyo Bay Maihama Hotel First Resort**:
    - **Why Choose This?** As an official Tokyo Disney Resort hotel, it provides convenient access to the parks while maintaining affordable pricing.
    - **Added Perks:** Themed rooms and shuttle service to the parks add to the appeal.

- **Budget Consideration:** Rates starting at ¥20,000 per night make this a solid choice for mid-range budgets.

Budget Stays

For travelers who want to experience the magic of Tokyo Disneyland without spending too much, there are budget-friendly options available.

- **Hostels and Guesthouses:**
    - **Why Choose This?** Hostels in nearby towns like Funabashi or Chiba offer affordable accommodations with basic amenities.
    - **Added Perks:** Many hostels offer free Wi-Fi, shared kitchens, and opportunities to connect with other travelers.
    - **Budget Consideration:** Dormitory beds start at approximately ¥3,000 per night, while private rooms can range from ¥5,000 to ¥8,000.
- **Airbnb or Vacation Rentals:**
    - **Why Choose This?** Renting an apartment or house can be an economical option, especially for families or groups.

- **Added Perks:** Enjoy more space, a kitchen for cooking meals, and a homey feel during your stay.
- **Budget Consideration:** Prices start at ¥10,000 per night and can vary depending on location and amenities.

- **Business Hotels:**
  - **Why Choose This?** Simple and efficient, business hotels near the parks, like those in Maihama or Urayasu, provide clean rooms and basic services.
  - **Added Perks:** Some hotels include complimentary breakfast or shuttles to the parks.
  - **Budget Consideration:** Rates typically range from ¥7,000 to ¥12,000 per night, making them a great choice for budget-conscious travelers.

Tips for Choosing the Right Accommodation

1. **Prioritize Convenience:** If your primary goal is easy access to the parks, consider on-site Disney hotels or nearby options along the Disney Resort Line.

2. **Book Early:** Tokyo Disneyland is an incredibly popular destination, and accommodations fill up fast, especially during peak seasons like holidays or school breaks.

3. **Consider Group Size:** Traveling with a large family or group? opt for accommodations that offer family rooms or vacation rentals to maximize comfort and savings.

4. **Check for Packages:** Many hotels, including on-site Disney hotels, offer packages that include park tickets or meal plans, which can simplify your planning.

5. **Factor in Transportation:** Budget options farther from the park may seem cheaper, but transportation costs can add up. Consider the total expense when choosing your stay.

With so many options available, Tokyo Disneyland has accommodations to suit every traveler's needs and budget. Whether you're looking for a luxurious escape, a mid-range stay with all the essentials, or a budget-friendly base for your adventure, there's a perfect place waiting for you.

Park Overview

Welcome to the magical realm of Tokyo Disneyland, where dreams come alive, and every step brings a new adventure. Let me take you on an immersive journey through the park's rich history and its incredible themed lands. As someone who has spent over two decades exploring its wonders, I'll share details, stories, and insider knowledge that will make your visit unforgettable.

History and Legacy of Tokyo Disneyland

Tokyo Disneyland's story begins in the late 1970s when The Walt Disney Company and The Oriental Land Company envisioned creating a Disney Park in Japan. Unlike its counterparts in the United States, this park would reflect Japanese culture's deep respect for hospitality, precision, and storytelling.

When the park opened on **April 15, 1983**, it was groundbreaking. Not only was it Disney's first park outside the United States, but it was also a bold step in blending American pop culture with Japanese sensibilities. The collaboration between Disney's Imagineers and Japanese architects resulted in a park that felt both globally magical and uniquely local.

The response was overwhelming. Tokyo Disneyland welcomed over **10 million guests in its first year** a record-breaking achievement. Over the decades, it has continued to evolve, introducing iconic attractions like Splash Mountain and Space Mountain, while remaining a timeless destination for families and fans.

One thing that sets Tokyo Disneyland apart is its **dedication to perfection**. Everything, from the meticulously landscaped gardens to the synchronized parades, speaks to the Japanese culture's pursuit of excellence. Cast Members go out of their way to make guests feel special, whether through a warm smile or helping you find the perfect souvenir.

In 2001, the resort expanded with **Tokyo DisneySea**, a park that complements Disneyland's whimsy with a more sophisticated, sea-themed adventure. Together, they form Tokyo Disney Resort, which attracts millions annually and continues to set the standard for theme park experiences worldwide.

Themed Lands Overview

The magic of Tokyo Disneyland is divided into seven themed lands, each with its own unique charm and storytelling. Let's explore these lands in detail.

World Bazaar

The moment you step into Tokyo Disneyland, you're greeted by the enchanting World Bazaar. Unlike Main Street, U.S.A., in other Disney parks, this area is covered by a grand glass canopy a thoughtful design to protect guests from Japan's unpredictable weather.

The architecture evokes a nostalgic feel, with gas lamps lining the streets and storefronts adorned with Victorian-era details. It's a place where the old-world charm of early 20th-century America comes alive. Strolling through World Bazaar, you'll notice something unique: this isn't just a shopping districtit's a gateway to the park's story.

- **Must-Visit Highlights**:
    - **Emporium**: The largest store in the park, offering everything from Mickey ears to exclusive Tokyo Disneyland merchandise.

- **Restaurant Hokusai**: A delightful mix of Japanese and Western cuisine, perfect for those looking to enjoy a sit-down meal.

World Bazaar's canopy also makes it a prime viewing spot for parades, especially during the rainy season. Grab a snack, find a spot, and let the magic unfold.

Adventureland

Adventureland is where the spirit of exploration comes to life. Divided into two sections **New Orleans Square** and **Jungle** it offers a mix of exotic landscapes, lively music, and thrilling attractions.

- **Key Attractions**:
  - **Pirates of the Caribbean**: Sail through dimly lit caverns filled with singing pirates, gold-filled treasure chests, and the mischievous Captain Jack Sparrow.
  - **Jungle Cruise**: This is not just a boat ride; it's a hilarious guided tour through a lush jungle with animatronic animals and a skipper who delivers the most delightfully corny jokes.

Adventureland also hosts unique dining options:

- **Blue Bayou Restaurant**: Located inside Pirates of the Caribbean, it offers an unforgettable experience of dining under "starlit" skies with lantern-lit tables.

Westernland

The American frontier comes alive in Westernland, Tokyo Disneyland's version of Frontierland. As you enter, you're greeted by rustic wooden facades, the sound of harmonicas, and the hum of a steamboat's whistle.

- **Key Attractions**:
    - **Big Thunder Mountain Railroad**: A high-speed mine train ride through red rock canyons and abandoned gold mines. The storytelling and theming here are immaculate, with every detail enhancing the sense of adventure.
    - **Mark Twain Riverboat**: For a calmer experience, step aboard this majestic paddle steamer for a scenic tour of the Rivers of America.

Westernland is also home to **Country Bear Theater**, a charming and humorous animatronic show featuring singing bears in a country-western setting.

Critter Country

Tucked away along the Rivers of America, Critter Country feels like stepping into a storybook. The rustic cabins, flowing streams, and cheerful critters create an inviting atmosphere that's both whimsical and adventurous.

- **Key Attractions**:
  - **Splash Mountain**: One of the park's most iconic rides, this log-flume adventure tells the tale of Br'er Rabbit's escapades. The final drop is exhilarating, and the views from the top are breathtaking.

For a quieter moment, consider renting a canoe at **Beaver Brothers Explorer Canoes** and paddling along the river.

Fantasyland

If there's one land that captures the heart of Disney's storytelling, it's Fantasyland. Dominated by the majestic **Cinderella Castle**, this is where fairy tales come to life.

- **Key Attractions**:
    - **Peter Pan's Flight**: Glide over London and Neverland in a magical pirate ship.
    - **It's a Small World**: This classic attraction recently received updates to include characters from Disney films, making it even more enchanting.
    - **Enchanted Tale of Beauty and the Beast**: A newer addition, this ride brings Belle's story to life with breathtaking animatronics and immersive scenes.

Fantasyland is also home to charming dining options like **Queen of Hearts Banquet Hall**, a whimsical restaurant inspired by *Alice in Wonderland*.

Toontown

Toontown is pure fun a vibrant, zany world where Disney characters live. This land is a paradise for younger visitors, but its playful design is sure to bring out the kid in everyone.

- **Key Attractions**:

- **Mickey's House and Meet Mickey**: Step into Mickey's world and snap a photo with the beloved mouse himself.

- **Roger Rabbit's Car Toon Spin**: A wild ride through Roger Rabbit's animated world.

Toontown's interactive elements like pulling levers or opening wacky doors make it a playground for imagination.

Tomorrowland

Tomorrowland is where innovation meets imagination. It's a sleek, futuristic land filled with thrilling attractions and interactive experiences.

- **Key Attractions**:
  - **Space Mountain**: This high-speed journey through the cosmos is a must for adrenaline seekers.

  - **Buzz Lightyear's Astro Blasters**: A family-friendly ride where you can shoot targets and compete for the highest score.

The land also features cutting-edge dining options like **Pan Galactic Pizza Port**, which serves creative, futuristic-themed dishes.

As you explore these lands, you'll realize that Tokyo Disneyland is not just a theme park it's a world meticulously crafted to spark joy and wonder. Each land tells its own story, inviting you to be part of the magic. Let's continue the journey as we uncover even more about this incredible place.

Must-See Rides and Experiences

Tokyo Disneyland boasts a plethora of attractions, each offering a unique blend of excitement, storytelling, and immersive environments. Let's explore some of the top experiences you simply can't miss.

1. Enchanted Tale of Beauty and the Beast

Step into the enchanting world of Belle and the Beast in this state-of-the-art attraction. Opened in 2020, it has quickly become a guest favorite, renowned for its groundbreaking technology and immersive storytelling.

- **Experience Highlights**:
    - **Trackless Ride System**: Glide seamlessly through the Beast's castle in enchanted dishes, experiencing a dance that mirrors the iconic ballroom scene.
    - **Animatronics**: Witness lifelike figures of Belle, the Beast, and other beloved characters, bringing the tale as old as time to vivid life.

- **Musical Score**: Be serenaded by the film's memorable songs, enhancing the emotional depth of the journey.
- **Pro Tip**: This attraction is immensely popular. Utilize the park's Fast Pass system or arrive early to secure a spot with minimal wait time.

2. Pooh's Hunny Hunt

Unique to Tokyo Disneyland, Pooh's Hunny Hunt is a whimsical adventure through the Hundred Acre Wood, celebrated for its innovative design and charming narrative.

- **Experience Highlights**:
  - **Trackless Ride Technology**: Enjoy a different experience each time as your honey pot takes unpredictable paths, creating a sense of spontaneity and wonder.
  - **Immersive Scenes**: Join Winnie the Pooh in his quest for honey, encountering friends like Tigger, Piglet, and Eeyore along the way.
  - **Interactive Elements**: Feel the bounce with Tigger and float through a dreamlike Heffalump and Woozle sequence, engaging all your senses.

- **Pro Tip**: Given its popularity, consider visiting during early park hours or using the Fast Pass option to reduce wait times.

3. Big Thunder Mountain

For those craving a rush of adrenaline, Big Thunder Mountain offers a thrilling ride through a haunted gold mine aboard a runaway train.

- **Experience Highlights**:
    - **Scenic Landscapes**: Race through detailed canyons, tunnels, and caverns, with each twist and turn revealing new surprises.
    - **Dynamic Ride Experience**: The combination of speed, sudden drops, and sharp turns keeps riders on the edge of their seats.
    - **Thematic Storytelling**: Immerse yourself in the lore of the cursed mining town, with atmospheric effects enhancing the adventure.
- **Pro Tip**: Evening rides offer a different ambiance, with the attraction illuminated against the night sky, providing a unique perspective.

4. Pirates of the Caribbean

Set sail on a swashbuckling voyage through pirate-infested waters in this classic attraction that combines storytelling with immersive environments.

- **Experience Highlights**:
    - **Detailed Sets**: Navigate through scenes of pirate raids, treasure troves, and coastal villages, each meticulously crafted.
    - **Animatronics**: Encounter lifelike pirates, including the infamous Captain Jack Sparrow, adding a touch of cinematic flair.
    - **Atmospheric Effects**: From cannon blasts to the smell of gunpowder, the multisensory elements draw you deeper into the adventure.
- **Pro Tip**: This ride typically has shorter wait times during parades and nighttime shows, making it an ideal choice during those periods.

5. Space Mountain

Blast off into the cosmos on Space Mountain, a high-speed indoor roller coaster that takes you on a thrilling journey through outer space.

- **Experience Highlights**:
    - **Darkness Ride**: The absence of light heightens the sensation of speed and unpredictability, amplifying the thrill factor.
    - **Futuristic Design**: The sleek, space-age aesthetic sets the tone for an interstellar adventure.
    - **Synchronized Soundtrack**: Dynamic music scores enhance the ride's intensity, syncing with the twists and turns.
- **Pro Tip**: For a more exhilarating experience, request a seat towards the back of the coaster, where the forces feel more pronounced.

6. It's a Small World with Groot

In 2025, Tokyo Disneyland introduced a limited-time overlay to the beloved "It's a Small World" attraction, featuring characters from the Marvel Cinematic Universe, notably Groot.

- **Experience Highlights**:
  - **Marvel Integration**: Spot miniature versions of Marvel heroes, seamlessly blended into the classic scenes, adding a new layer of excitement.
  - **Musical Variations**: Enjoy subtle musical nods to Marvel themes intertwined with the iconic "It's a Small World" melody.
  - **Visual Enhancements**: Updated sets and costumes reflect the Marvel universe, providing a fresh take on the timeless ride.
- **Pro Tip**: This overlay is available from January 15 to June 30, 2025. Be sure to experience it during this window, as such limited-time offerings are rare and highly anticipated.

7. Splash Mountain

Join Br'er Rabbit on a lively adventure through the briar patch, culminating in a thrilling five-story drop that promises a refreshing splash.

- **Experience Highlights**:
  - **Engaging Storyline**: Follow the mischievous Br'er Rabbit as he seeks

adventure, encountering various characters along the way.

- o **Immersive Animatronics**: From cheerful critters to Br'er Fox's sly antics, the scenes are filled with lively characters and vibrant details.

- o **The Grand Finale**: The climactic drop offers breathtaking views of the park before plunging you into the refreshing splash below.

- **Pro Tip**: Consider riding Splash Mountain during the warmer months to cool off, and aim for the front row if you don't mind getting wet!

8. Buzz Lightyear's Astro Blasters

Calling all Space Rangers! Join Buzz Lightyear in this interactive ride that combines fun, competition, and a chance to save the galaxy.

- **Experience Highlights**:

  - o **Interactive Gameplay**: Use your laser blaster to hit targets and rack up points as you fight against Emperor Zurg and his minions.

  - o **Colorful Set Design**: Each scene pops with vibrant colors, bringing the world of Toy Story to life.

- o **Replayability**: Compete with friends or family to see who earns the highest score it's a ride you'll want to do again and again.
- **Pro Tip**: Aim for the Z-shaped targets, as they often yield higher points. The ride is especially fun at night when the lines tend to be shorter.

9. Monsters, Inc. Ride & Go Seek

Step into the whimsical world of Monstropolis with this one-of-a-kind interactive dark ride.

- **Experience Highlights**:
    - o **Flashlight Gameplay**: Use a provided flashlight to "find" Boo and interact with various characters from *Monsters, Inc.* as the story unfolds.
    - o **Lifelike Animatronics**: Sulley, Mike, and other familiar faces appear in stunningly realistic forms.
    - o **Family-Friendly Fun**: The ride is gentle enough for kids but engaging enough to keep adults entertained.
- **Pro Tip**: Early mornings or late evenings are the best times to experience this attraction with shorter wait times.

10. Haunted Mansion

Prepare for a spooky, but family-friendly, adventure through a haunted estate filled with ghosts, ghouls, and playful spirits.

- **Experience Highlights**:
    - **Detailed Storytelling**: From the stretching room to the ballroom filled with dancing phantoms, each scene tells a part of the mansion's eerie tale.
    - **Spectacular Effects**: From floating candelabras to ghostly projections, the mansion is a masterpiece of Disney's special effects.
    - **Seasonal Variants**: During Halloween and Christmas, the ride transforms with a *Nightmare Before Christmas* overlay.
- **Pro Tip**: Visit during the holiday season for a unique twist on this classic attraction, but expect slightly longer waits.

11. Jungle Cruise

Embark on a lighthearted river adventure through exotic landscapes filled with animatronic animals, ancient ruins, and plenty of humor.

- **Experience Highlights**:
  - **Charismatic Skippers**: Your guide will entertain you with puns, jokes, and playful storytelling, making each cruise unique.
  - **Immersive Environment**: From lush greenery to cascading waterfalls, the attention to detail is stunning.
  - **After Dark**: The nighttime version of the Jungle Cruise offers a slightly spookier atmosphere, adding a new layer to the adventure.
- **Pro Tip**: Sit closer to the skipper if you want to catch all the jokes!

12. Peter Pan's Flight

Soar over London and Neverland in a magical pirate ship that brings one of Disney's most beloved stories to life.

- **Experience Highlights**:
  - **Flight Simulation**: Suspended tracks make you feel like you're truly flying, with breathtaking aerial views of iconic scenes.
  - **Charming Animations**: Watch as Peter, Wendy, and Tinker Bell

outsmart Captain Hook in beautifully crafted tableaus.

- o **Timeless Appeal**: This ride is a must for anyone who cherishes the classic Disney films.

- **Pro Tip**: Peter Pan's Flight is one of the park's most popular attractions head there first thing in the morning to avoid long lines.

13. Toontown's Mickey's House and Meet Mickey

This isn't just a meet-and-greet it's an entire experience in Mickey's whimsical home.

- **Experience Highlights**:
  - o **Interactive Spaces**: Explore Mickey's kitchen, living room, and even his movie studio, each filled with playful, cartoonish details.
  - o **Character Encounter**: Meet Mickey Mouse himself and snap a photo with the beloved icon.
  - o **Perfect for Kids**: Younger visitors especially adore this chance to see Mickey in his element.

- **Pro Tip**: Arrive early to avoid long lines for meeting Mickey this is a popular stop for families.

14. The Castle's Grand Adventure

While Cinderella Castle is the centerpiece of Fantasyland, it's also an experience in itself. Inside, you'll find exhibits, photo spots, and even a few surprises.

- **Experience Highlights**:
    - **Castle Walkthrough**: Discover murals, stained glass windows, and exhibits that tell Cinderella's story.
    - **Magical Photo Ops**: Snap pictures from balconies with stunning views of the park.
    - **Special Events**: Occasionally, the castle hosts seasonal displays or interactive exhibits.
- **Pro Tip**: Check the park schedule to see if there are any unique events happening at the castle during your visit.

15. Seasonal Events and Pop-Up Activities

Tokyo Disneyland is famous for its seasonal overlays, special parades, and limited-time activities. From the **Easter Egg Hunt**

Adventure to the **Disney Halloween Parade**, each event brings new life to the park.

- **Pro Tip**: Keep an eye on the park's event calendar to make sure you don't miss out on these exciting experiences.

With so many thrilling and enchanting attractions, Tokyo Disneyland promises something special for everyone. From adrenaline-pumping rides to whimsical adventures, your journey through this magical park will be packed with unforgettable moments. Be sure to plan your day wisely to make the most of every experience!

New Attractions for 2025

Tokyo Disneyland in 2025 is gearing up for an extraordinary year, offering guests cutting-edge new attractions that will immerse you in thrilling worlds and unforgettable adventures. I can confidently say these upcoming experiences are unlike anything we've seen before. Let's dive deep into the details.

"It's a Small World with Groot"

What happens when a Marvel favorite meets one of Disney's most iconic attractions? Pure magic! For a limited time, *it's a Small World* will feature a charming overlay with Groot, blending the classic ride's global message of unity with the fun and humor of the Marvel universe.

Why It's a Must-See: *It's a Small World* has always been a heartwarming journey through cultures and countries. Adding Groot to the mix brings a fresh layer of excitement and curiosity. Whether you're a lifelong fan of the Guardians of the Galaxy or just love spotting new details in classic attractions, this overlay will leave you smiling.

- **Experience Highlights:**
    - **Groot's Adventure:** Groot embarks on a global journey, appearing in various scenes alongside the ride's iconic dolls. From a samba-filled party in South America to a serene cherry blossom garden in Japan, Groot seamlessly joins the celebration of diversity.
    - **Musical Mashup:** The ride's signature tune remains intact but is creatively remixed with whimsical nods to the *Guardians of the Galaxy* soundtrack. It's subtle yet delightful listen closely for these Easter eggs!
    - **Interactive Elements:** Keep an eye out for hidden Groot figures tucked into the ride's scenery. These playful surprises add an extra layer of engagement, especially for Marvel fans.

Insider Insights:

- *Timing is Everything:* The overlay runs from **January 15 to June 30, 2025**. Arrive early or use Disney's Premier Access (formerly FastPass) to secure your spotthis limited-time experience is bound to attract crowds.

- *Best Views:* Sit in the middle rows of the boat for a balanced view of the updated scenes on both sides.

- *Extra Fun:* Check out the special *It's a Small World with Groot* merchandise and snacks in nearby shops. The Groot-shaped popcorn bucket is already creating buzz!

Upcoming Wreck-It Ralph Attraction

Fans of *Wreck-It Ralph*, get ready: Tomorrowland is welcoming a brand-new attraction inspired by the beloved film. Though set to open in **fiscal year 2026**, the buzz surrounding this ride is already palpable, with construction underway and concept art teasing an incredible adventure.

What We Know So Far: The new *Wreck-It Ralph* attraction promises to transport guests directly into the vibrant world of Ralph and Vanellope. From the digital chaos of Ralph's arcade games to the candy-coated wonderland of Sugar Rush, this ride is shaping up to be an instant classic.

- **Ride Highlights:**
    - **Interactive Gameplay:** Guests will be active participants, helping Ralph and Vanellope fix a world disrupted by mischievous "Sugar Bugs." Imagine firing digital "code streams" to repair glitches and restore order it's as if you're inside a video game!
    - **Immersive Environments:** The ride will combine physical sets and digital screens, making the transition between Ralph's arcade and Sugar Rush seamless and spectacular. Expect dazzling visuals, vibrant colors, and an overload of sweet details.
    - **Family-Friendly Fun:** This attraction is designed to delight guests of all ages, offering a mix of fast-paced action and whimsical humor.

What Sets It Apart: Tokyo Disneyland is known for creating one-of-a-kind attractions, and this *Wreck-It Ralph* ride is no exception. The integration of interactive technology ensures that every visit feels unique, much like the trackless system in *Pooh's Hunny Hunt*.

Tips for Future Visitors:

- **Anticipation Strategy:** Since this ride will replace *Buzz Lightyear's Astro Blasters* (which closed in October 2024), expect high demand once it opens. Keep an eye on announcements for soft opening previews.

- **Queue Entertainment:** If the concept art is any indication, even waiting in line will be a treat, with interactive displays and retro arcade nods to entertain you.

- **Exclusive Additions:** Rumor has it there will be themed dining options nearby, offering Sugar Rush-inspired treats like colorful cupcakes and milkshakes.

These new attractions highlight what makes Tokyo Disneyland so exceptional: its ability to blend nostalgia with innovation. Whether it's Groot dancing through *It's a Small World* or Ralph pulling you into his pixelated chaos, these experiences promise to surprise, delight, and immerse you like never before.

Here's what excites me most: Both attractions reflect the park's commitment to storytelling. They're not just rides; they're adventures that put you right in the heart of the action. So, as you plan your trip, make room in your itinerary for these upcoming gems they're worth every second.

Special Shows and Parades

When you visit Tokyo Disneyland, you'll find yourself immersed in a world of live entertainment that elevates the magic of the park to extraordinary levels. I can confidently say that the parades and shows here are among the best in the world. These aren't just spectacles they're emotional, uplifting, and unforgettable experiences. Let me take you through the highlights of Tokyo Disneyland's special shows and parades.

1. Disney Harmony in Color

Tokyo Disneyland's newest daytime parade, *Disney Harmony in Color*, is a vibrant celebration of adventure, family, and friendship. Premiering in 2023, this parade continues to captivate visitors with its colorful floats, lively performances, and heartwarming stories.

What to Expect

- **Storytelling in Motion**: Each float represents a beloved Disney movie, from *Moana* and *Coco* to *Zootopia* and *Frozen 2*. The parade seamlessly transitions between these stories, with performers bringing the characters to life.

- **A Symphony of Color**: The floats are not just decorations they are moving works of art. Every detail, from the shimmering fabrics to the hand-painted designs, is meticulously crafted.

- **An Uplifting Score**: The music is a medley of Disney classics reimagined for this parade, perfectly complementing each float's theme.

Insider Tips

- **Best Viewing Spots**: The Central Plaza in front of Cinderella Castle offers a prime viewing location. Arrive at least 30 minutes early to secure a spot.

- **Interactive Moments**: Performers often engage with the crowd, waving, dancing, and creating magical moments for guests especially those in the front rows.

2. Tokyo Disneyland Electrical Parade

The *DreamLights* parade is nothing short of spectacular. As the sun sets, the park transforms into a glowing wonderland, and this nighttime parade takes center stage with its dazzling lights and unforgettable soundtrack.

What to Expect

- **Luminous Floats**: Each float is adorned with thousands of LED lights, creating an ethereal glow. Look out for Cinderella's shimmering carriage, Buzz Lightyear's high-tech spaceship, and Mickey's glowing steamboat.

- **Beloved Characters**: From classic Disney royalty to Pixar favorites, you'll see a wide variety of characters. Each float is a unique tribute to the stories and personalities we all love.

- **Musical Masterpiece**: The parade's soundtrack is a mix of orchestral Disney tunes and modern adaptations, perfectly timed with the floats' movements and lighting.

Insider Tips

- **Best Timing**: Plan to watch the second performance of *DreamLights* (if available) for smaller crowds and a quieter atmosphere.

- **Pro Photo Tip**: Use a slower shutter speed on your camera or phone to capture the glowing trails of light from the floats.

3. Mickey's Magical Music World

Housed in the grand **Fantasyland Forest Theatre**, this live show is a feast for the senses. It's a Broadway-style production featuring Mickey Mouse and his friends as they explore the power of music.

What to Expect

- **Elaborate Sets**: The stage transforms seamlessly between iconic Disney settings, including the Pride Lands from *The Lion King* and the underwater world of *The Little Mermaid*.

- **Live Performances**: The cast of dancers, singers, and costumed characters deliver an energetic performance filled with laughter, emotion, and surprises.

- **Musical Variety**: From ballads to upbeat dance numbers, the music spans a range of Disney classics that will have you humming along.

Insider Tips

- **Reservations**: Seats are limited, so use the Tokyo Disneyland app to reserve your spot early in the day.

- **Family-Friendly**: The theater is air-conditioned, making it a perfect mid-day break for families with young children.

4. Vanellope's Sweet Pop World (Seasonal Parade)

Running from **January 15 to March 16, 2025**, *Vanellope's Sweet Pop World* is a limited-time parade that immerses guests in the candy-coated universe of *Wreck-It Ralph*.

What to Expect

- **Sugar Rush Floats**: Each float is a sugary spectacle, featuring candy-colored landscapes, giant cupcakes, and sparkling lollipops. Vanellope von Schweetz herself takes center stage, joined by Ralph and other characters.

- **Interactive Fun**: Performers toss candy-shaped confetti into the crowd, while Vanellope's float sprays bubbles, adding a playful element to the parade.

- **Pop-Inspired Music**: The soundtrack is upbeat and irresistibly catchy, blending tracks from *Wreck-It Ralph* with new compositions.

Insider Tips

- **Best Spot**: Line up near World Bazaar for the chance to see the floats up close as they emerge from backstage.

- **Limited Merchandise**: Look for exclusive *Vanellope's Sweet Pop World* souvenirs, such as themed popcorn buckets and plush toys.

5. Seasonal Highlights

One of the best things about Tokyo Disneyland is its dedication to seasonal celebrations. Each season brings unique parades and shows that add fresh excitement to your visit.

Disney Halloween Parade

- **Spooky Meets Whimsy**: Disney villains join the parade in a fun and family-friendly celebration of Halloween.

- **Costume Extravaganza**: Cast Members and performers wear Halloween-themed costumes that blend Disney charm with spooky details.

- **Pro Tip**: Attend in costume! During Halloween season, guests are allowed to wear full Disney character costumes.

Disney Christmas Stories

- **Holiday Magic**: This Christmas parade features festive floats with twinkling lights, snow effects, and appearances from Santa Claus alongside Mickey and Minnie.

- **Caroling Atmosphere**: The parade's soundtrack features heartwarming renditions of holiday classics.

6. Stage Shows

Tokyo Disneyland offers an array of stage shows that combine storytelling, music, and Disney's signature magic.

The Enchanted Tiki Room: Stitch Presents "Aloha E Komo Mai!"

- **What to Expect**: Stitch brings his playful antics to this tropical show, adding humor and Hawaiian-inspired songs to the Tiki Room experience.

- **Insider Tip**: This show is a great option for families looking to relax in a shaded, air-conditioned setting.

7. Nighttime Spectacle: Reach for the Stars

These fireworks show, introduced in 2024, is a breathtaking conclusion to your day at Tokyo Disneyland.

What to Expect

- **Castle Projections**: Cinderella Castle becomes the centerpiece, with stunning projections that sync perfectly with the music.

- **Fireworks Display**: The pyrotechnics light up the sky in a dazzling array of colors and patterns.

- **Emotional Soundtrack**: The music tells a story of dreams, determination, and magic.

Insider Tips

- **Where to Watch**: The Central Plaza provides the best view, but you can also enjoy the fireworks from Tomorrowland for a unique angle.

- **Plan Ahead**: Check the weather forecast, as fireworks may be canceled on windy nights.

Tokyo Disneyland's parades and shows are more than just entertainment they're integral parts of the park's magic. Whether it's the vibrant floats of *Harmony in Color*, the glow of *DreamLights*, or the spectacle of *Reach for the Stars*, each show and parade offer a new way to experience the wonder of Disney.

Hidden Gems and Underrated Experiences

When visiting Tokyo Disneyland, it's easy to focus on the big-name attractions Space Mountain, Big Thunder Mountain, and Splash Mountain, to name a few. But there's a world of magic waiting for those willing to venture off the beaten path. Let's explore the enchanting corners of Tokyo Disneyland that you may not have noticed before.

1. The Secret Path to Serenity: The Westernland River Trail

Nestled alongside the Rivers of America in Westernland is a peaceful trail that feels miles away from the hustle and bustle of the park. This quiet path offers a scenic stroll with stunning views of the Mark Twain Riverboat and Tom Sawyer Island.

What Makes It Special

- **Tranquility in the Park**: This hidden gem is perfect for those moments when you need a breather. It's shaded, quiet, and offers benches where you can sit and soak in the atmosphere.

- **Photo Opportunities**: The river trail provides picturesque views of the river, boats, and surrounding nature perfect for capturing magical memories.

Pro Tip

- Visit this area during sunset for a stunning golden glow on the water. It's one of the most serene spots in the park.

2. Tom Sawyer Island: A World of Exploration

While many guests rush past this charming island, it's a must-visit for families and explorers alike. Accessible by raft, Tom Sawyer Island is a playground of adventure, featuring caves, rope bridges, and hidden treasures.

What Makes It Special

- **Interactive Fun**: From discovering secret passages in Injun Joe's Cave to crossing wobbly suspension bridges, every corner of the island invites exploration.

- **A Break from the Crowds**: The island tends to be less crowded than other areas of the park, giving you space to roam freely.

Pro Tip

- Pack a snack or drink and enjoy a quiet picnic while watching the riverboats pass by.

3. The Harmony of the Hub Gardens

While most guests head straight for the attractions, the beautifully landscaped Hub Gardens in front of Cinderella Castle often go unnoticed. These themed gardens change with the seasons, offering a quiet place to relax.

What Makes It Special

- **Seasonal Displays**: From cherry blossoms in spring to festive Christmas lights in winter, the gardens are always a feast for the eyes.

- **A Perfect Picnic Spot**: Pick up a snack from nearby World Bazaar and enjoy the scenery.

Pro Tip

- Look out for hidden Disney character sculptures and details in the flower beds they make for great photo ops!

4. The Enchanted Tiki Room: Stitch Presents "Aloha E Komo Mai!"

The Tiki Room is often overshadowed by thrill rides, but this delightful show featuring Stitch is a tropical escape filled with humor and heartwarming songs.

What Makes It Special

- **Stitch's Antics**: The mischievous alien adds a playful twist to the classic Tiki Room experience, making it a hit with kids and adults alike.
- **Catchy Tunes**: You'll find yourself humming "Aloha E Komo Mai" long after the show ends.

Pro Tip

- Visit during the hottest part of the day to enjoy the air-conditioned comfort and escape the midday heat.

5. Mickey's PhilharMagic: A Musical Journey

Located in Fantasyland, this 4D musical experience takes you on a whirlwind tour through some of Disney's most beloved songs, led by none other than Donald Duck.

What Makes It Special

- **Immersive Technology**: From scents to wind effects, the 4D experience makes you feel like you're part of the action.

- **Beloved Music**: Relive the magic of classics like *The Little Mermaid*'s "Part of Your World" and *Aladdin*'s "A Whole New World."

Pro Tip

- Sit in the middle rows for the best perspective and to fully enjoy the 4D effects.

6. Critter Country's Beaver Brothers Explorer Canoes

Hidden away in Critter Country is an interactive attraction where you can paddle your own canoe along the Rivers of America. It's an activity often overlooked by visitors rushing to Splash Mountain.

What Makes It Special

- **Interactive Fun**: You and your fellow guests will work together to paddle the canoe, making it a unique, hands-on experience.

- **Unique Views**: From the water, you'll see the park from a perspective few other attractions offer.

Pro Tip

- Go early in the day to avoid the heat, as this attraction is outdoors and can be physically demanding.

7. The World Bazaar Roof Mosaics

At first glance, World Bazaar seems like a typical shopping district, but if you look closer especially upwards you'll notice intricate mosaics on the glass ceiling panels. These are beautiful works of art, often missed by hurried guests.

What Makes It Special

- **Hidden Beauty**: The roof mosaics depict subtle scenes of magic and nostalgia, adding a touch of wonder to the marketplace.

- **A Quiet Escape**: World Bazaar is a great spot to linger, particularly on rainy days when the glass canopy shields you from the elements.

Pro Tip

- Visit during the evening when the soft lighting highlights the mosaics, creating a warm and magical ambiance.

8. Tomorrowland's Cosmic-themed Snacks

While most visitors head straight for Space Mountain, the food in Tomorrowland is a hidden gem that deserves attention. Themed snacks like alien mochi and Star Wars-inspired beverages are a treat for the senses.

What Makes It Special

- **Unique Flavors**: From matcha to custard-filled mochi, these treats are both delicious and photogenic.//
- **Exclusive Offerings**: Many of these snacks are unique to Tokyo Disneyland, making them a must-try for foodies.

Pro Tip

- Pair your snack with a quick ride on the Tomorrowland Transit Speedway for a relaxing break.

9. The Secret Photo Spots

While everyone lines up for pictures in front of Cinderella Castle, there are quieter photo spots scattered throughout the park that offer equally stunning backdrops.

What Makes It Special

- **Unique Angles**: Capture the castle from the bridge to Adventureland or the lush gardens near Critter Country for less crowded, equally enchanting photos.
- **Hidden Details**: Look for smaller, themed props around the park, like vintage luggage in World Bazaar or pirate gear in Adventureland.

Pro Tip

- Early morning or late evening light creates the best natural lighting for photos.

10. The Cinderella Castle Walkthrough

Most visitors admire Cinderella Castle from the outside, but the walkthrough experience inside the castle is a hidden treasure many overlook.

What Makes It Special

- **Fairy Tale Magic**: Explore murals, dioramas, and exhibits that retell the story of Cinderella with breathtaking artistry.

- **Panoramic Views**: The upper floors provide incredible views of Fantasyland and beyond.

Pro Tip

- Visit during quieter hours to have more time to explore the intricate details without the crowds.

While Tokyo Disneyland's major attractions are undeniably magical, these hidden gems and underrated experiences add layers of charm and depth to your visit. They invite you to slow down, notice the details, and connect with the park in unexpected ways. Whether it's paddling a canoe, discovering mosaics in World Bazaar, or exploring

Tom Sawyer Island, these moments will make your trip truly unforgettable.

Cultural Insights

Tokyo Disneyland is a harmonious blend of Disney magic and Japanese culture, creating a unique experience that delights visitors from around the world. As you prepare for your adventure, understanding the cultural nuances and seasonal celebrations can enrich your visit. Let's explore how Japanese traditions and etiquette intertwine with the enchantment of Tokyo Disneyland.

Japanese Etiquette and Disney Magic

Japanese society places a high value on respect, politeness, and harmony. These principles are evident throughout Tokyo Disneyland, enhancing the park's welcoming atmosphere.

Queueing and Patience

In Japan, orderly queuing is a cultural norm, and this extends to the park's attractions. Guests wait patiently in line, maintaining a calm and respectful demeanor. This practice ensures a pleasant experience for everyone.

Cleanliness

You'll notice the park is impeccably clean, reflecting Japan's emphasis on tidiness. Guests are conscientious about disposing of trash properly, and you'll find designated smoking areas to maintain air quality.

Politeness

Cast Members (staff) exemplify Japanese hospitality, known as "omotenashi." Their courteous and attentive service adds a layer of warmth to your visit. A simple bow or "arigato" (thank you) in return is appreciated and reciprocates the respect.

Pro Tip: Embrace these cultural practices during your visit. Participating in the local etiquette enhances your experience and shows respect for Japanese customs.

Local Traditions Integrated into the Park

Tokyo Disneyland seamlessly incorporates Japanese traditions, offering a culturally rich experience alongside classic Disney attractions.

Seasonal Decorations

The park's decor changes with the seasons, reflecting traditional Japanese festivals and customs. During spring, cherry blossom motifs adorn the park, celebrating "hanami" (flower viewing). In autumn, you'll find decorations inspired by "momiji" (autumn leaves), showcasing the beauty of Japanese nature.

Cuisine

Japanese culinary traditions are well-represented in the park's dining options. From sushi and tempura to seasonal delicacies like "sakura" (cherry blossom) flavored treats in spring, the food offerings provide an authentic taste of Japan.

Cultural Performances

Traditional Japanese music and dance are often featured in the park's entertainment lineup. These performances offer insight into Japan's rich cultural heritage, adding depth to the Disney experience.

Pro Tip: Take time to explore these cultural elements. Enjoying local cuisine and attending traditional performances can provide a deeper appreciation of Japan's heritage.

Seasonal Events and Celebrations

Tokyo Disneyland hosts a variety of seasonal events that blend Disney magic with Japanese festivities. These celebrations offer unique experiences throughout the year.

New Year's Special Event

Celebrated from January 1 to January 13, the New Year's event at Tokyo Disneyland is a festive occasion that honors Japanese "Oshogatsu" (New Year) traditions.

Highlights:

- **Kadomatsu Decorations:** Traditional bamboo and pine decorations, known as "kadomatsu," are placed at the park's entrances to welcome the New Year.

- **Special Performances:** Exclusive shows featuring Disney characters dressed in traditional Japanese attire celebrate the spirit of the season.

- **Limited-Time Merchandise:** Unique New Year's-themed souvenirs are available, offering a chance to bring home a piece of the celebration.

Pro Tip: Visiting during the New Year's event provides an opportunity to experience Japanese cultural traditions firsthand, making your trip memorable and culturally enriching.

Disney Halloween

From September 17 to October 31, Tokyo Disneyland transforms into a Halloween wonderland, blending spooky fun with Japanese cultural nuances.

Highlights:

- **Halloween Parade:** A lively procession featuring Disney characters in Halloween costumes entertains guests with music and dance.

- **Themed Attractions:** Certain rides receive Halloween overlays, offering a unique twist to favorite experiences.

- **Costume Days:** On select days, guests are encouraged to dress up as their favorite Disney characters, adding to the festive atmosphere.

Pro Tip: Check the event schedule for "Costume Days" to participate in the fun. Remember to follow the park's guidelines for costumes to ensure a safe and enjoyable experience for all.

Disney Christmas

Celebrated from November 11 to December 25, Tokyo Disneyland's Christmas event combines Western holiday traditions with Japanese cultural elements, creating a unique festive atmosphere.

Highlights:

- **Christmas Parade:** A joyful parade featuring Disney characters in holiday attire spreads Christmas cheer throughout the park.

- **Seasonal Decorations:** The park is adorned with beautiful lights and ornaments, including displays that incorporate Japanese aesthetics.

- **Holiday Cuisine:** Special menus offer holiday-themed dishes and treats, blending Western and Japanese flavors.

Pro Tip: Evening visits during the Christmas season allow you to fully appreciate the illuminated decorations, creating a magical and heartwarming experience.

Experiencing Tokyo Disneyland through the lens of Japanese culture offers a unique and enriching adventure. By embracing local etiquette, appreciating the integration of traditions, and participating in seasonal events, you'll gain a deeper understanding of Japan's rich heritage while enjoying the timeless magic of Disney.

Dining and Shopping

Tokyo Disneyland isn't just about thrilling rides and magical attractions it's also a paradise for foodies and shopaholics. The park is packed with culinary delights and exclusive merchandise that will captivate your taste buds and tempt your wallet. I'll guide you through the must-try foods, immersive dining experiences, and hidden shopping gems that make this park truly one-of-a-kind.

Must-Try Foods and Snacks

Food at Tokyo Disneyland isn't just sustenance it's part of the adventure. The park's culinary offerings are as whimsical and magical as its attractions. Let's dig into some iconic and unique snacks you absolutely can't miss:

1. Mickey-Shaped Churros

A fan favorite, these churros are a playful twist on the classic treat. Warm, crispy, and coated in cinnamon sugar, the Mickey-shaped churros are as Instagram-worthy as they are delicious. Seasonal flavors, such as matcha or chocolate, occasionally make an appearance.

- **Where to Find It**: Snack carts in World Bazaar and Westernland.

- **Pro Tip**: The matcha-flavored churros are a must if you visit during spring!

2. Alien Mochi

Inspired by the adorable aliens from *Toy Story*, these chewy mochi dumplings are filled with custard, chocolate, or strawberry cream. Each piece is adorably decorated and surprisingly satisfying.

- **Where to Find It**: Tomorrowland's Pan Galactic Pizza Port.

- **Pro Tip**: They come in sets of three, making them perfect for sharingor not!

3. Popcorn Madness

Popcorn isn't just popcorn at Tokyo Disneylandit's a cultural experience. With unique flavors like soy sauce and butter, curry, honey, and caramel, there's a flavor for everyone. But the real star? The collectible popcorn buckets, which come in designs inspired by Disney characters and attractions.

- **Where to Find It**: Popcorn stands throughout the park.

- **Pro Tip**: The limited-edition popcorn buckets sell out fast, so grab one early in the day.

4. Gyoza Dog

This handheld treat is a steamed bun stuffed with juicy pork and vegetables. Soft, savory, and portable, it's perfect for a quick snack while you explore.

- **Where to Find It**: Tomorrowland Terrace.
- **Pro Tip**: Pair it with a drink from one of the specialty beverage carts nearby for a refreshing combo.

5. Seasonal Delights

Tokyo Disneyland celebrates every season with special menu items. During spring, you might find sakura (cherry blossom) mochi or desserts, while Halloween brings pumpkin-flavored treats and Christmas offers festive cakes and cookies.

- **Where to Find It**: Seasonal food carts and restaurants throughout the park.
- **Pro Tip**: Check the Tokyo Disneyland app to see the current seasonal menu offerings.

Themed Restaurants and Cafes

Dining at Tokyo Disneyland is more than just eating it's stepping into a story. Each restaurant immerses you in a uniquely themed world, where the atmosphere is as delightful as the food.

1. Queen of Hearts Banquet Hall

Step into the whimsical world of *Alice in Wonderland* at this elaborately themed restaurant. The decor features oversized playing cards, heart-shaped chandeliers, and nods to the Queen of Hearts herself.

- **What to Eat**: Roast beef platters, colorful desserts, and heart-shaped bread.
- **Pro Tip**: This restaurant is a visual feast, so be sure to take photos of the themed tableware and decor before you dig in.

2. Crystal Palace Restaurant

This elegant buffet-style restaurant offers a wide selection of international and Japanese cuisines. The glass-roofed building floods with natural light, making it a serene spot for a relaxing meal.

- **What to Eat**: Fresh sushi, pasta, and a dessert bar that's to die for.

- **Pro Tip**: Book a reservation early in the day using the Tokyo Disneyland app.

3. Grandma Sara's Kitchen

Nestled in Critter Country, this cozy spot feels like stepping into a woodland burrow. The rustic design and comforting Japanese meals make it a favorite for families.

- **What to Eat**: Curry rice, chicken teriyaki, and miso soup.
- **Pro Tip**: The tables near the windows offer great views of Splash Mountain.

4. Pan Galactic Pizza Port

Perfect for space explorers, this Tomorrowland restaurant serves creative, futuristic pizzas. The robotic chef, Tony Solaroni, adds an extra layer of fun to the dining experience.

- **What to Eat**: Shrimp and mayo pizza, sausage pizza, and alien mochi for dessert.
- **Pro Tip**: Watch the animatronic chef work his magic while you wait for your order.

5. Hungry Bear Restaurant

Located in Westernland, this spot offers hearty Japanese curry dishes in a rustic, frontier-themed setting.

- **What to Eat**: Pork cutlet curry or vegetable curry, served with rice.
- **Pro Tip**: Grab a seat by the river for a peaceful dining experience.

Shopping for Souvenirs and Merchandise

Shopping at Tokyo Disneyland is an experience in itself. The merchandise here is often exclusive, beautifully designed, and uniquely Japanese.

1. Mickey Ears with a Twist

Sure, you've seen Mickey ears before but Tokyo Disneyland takes them to the next level. From seasonal designs to limited-edition styles featuring cherry blossoms, Halloween themes, or Japanese motifs, there's a pair for every occasion.

- **Where to Buy**: Emporium in World Bazaar.

2. Japanese-Inspired Disney Merchandise

You'll find exclusive items that blend Disney magic with Japanese culture, like bento boxes featuring Mickey and Minnie, chopsticks adorned with Disney characters, and yukatas (light summer kimonos) with subtle Disney prints.

- **Where to Buy**: House of Greetings and Kingdom Treasures.

3. Limited-Edition Collectibles

Each season brings unique merchandise, such as plush toys, themed mugs, and decorative pins. During special events like Halloween or Christmas, you'll find items that are only available during that time of year.

- **Where to Buy**: Seasonal pop-up shops and specialty stores across the park.

4. Popcorn Buckets

These aren't just snack holders they're collectibles. Designs change frequently and often tie into new attractions or events. Think Cinderella's carriage, Buzz Lightyear's spaceship, or even a pumpkin-shaped bucket for Halloween.

- **Where to Buy**: Popcorn stands throughout the park.

- **Pro Tip**: Some buckets are exclusive to certain locations, so plan your hunt accordingly.

Seasonal Menus and Limited-Edition Items

Every season brings a new wave of culinary creativity to Tokyo Disneyland. From spring's cherry blossom-themed treats to winter's cozy holiday desserts, there's always something fresh and exciting to try.

Spring: Sakura Delights

- **What to Try**: Cherry blossom-flavored mochi, sakura soft serve, and pastel-colored macarons.

- **Pro Tip**: Pair these treats with a stroll through the cherry blossom-themed decorations in Fantasyland.

Summer: Cool Refreshments

- **What to Try**: Shaved ice with tropical fruit syrups, cold noodle dishes, and fruity popsicles.

- **Pro Tip**: Stay hydrated with the park's specialty mocktails, available at outdoor drink carts.

Autumn: Pumpkin Everything

- **What to Try**: Pumpkin churros, spiced lattes, and Halloween-themed cookies.

- **Pro Tip**: Visit during Disney Halloween for a chance to try spooky snacks that are only available for a few weeks.

Winter: Festive Feasts

- **What to Try**: Roasted turkey legs, Christmas cakes, and hot chocolate topped with Mickey-shaped marshmallows.

- **Pro Tip**: Look for holiday-themed dining packages that include exclusive keepsakes like plates or mugs.

At Tokyo Disneyland, food and shopping are integral to the experience. Whether you're savoring a Mickey-shaped churro or bringing home a one-of-a-kind souvenir, these moments add layers of joy to your adventure. So, indulge, explore, and let the magic guide your choices you'll treasure these memories long after you leave the park.

Suggested Itineraries

Planning your visit to Tokyo Disneyland is all about maximizing the magic and making every moment count. Whether you're there for one day or indulging in a multi-day adventure, I've crafted practical yet imaginative itineraries tailored to your travel style. With over 20 years of experience exploring every corner of this magical park, I'm here to guide you through the must-dos, hidden treasures, and pro tips for creating unforgettable memories.

One-Day Adventure Plan

If you have just one day, don't worry you can still experience the best of Tokyo Disneyland with a well-structured plan.

Morning: Hit the Ground Running

1. **Arrive Early**: The gates open at 8:00 AM (check the schedule), but aim to arrive at least 30 minutes before to beat the crowds.

2. **Start with a Thrill**: Head straight to **Space Mountain** in Tomorrowland. The lines build up quickly, and it's the perfect way to kick off your day with a rush of adrenaline.

3. **FastPass (Premier Access)**: Secure your spot for *Enchanted Tale of Beauty and the Beast*. This new attraction is wildly popular, and Premier Access ensures you won't miss out.

4. **Breakfast on the Go**: Grab a **Gyoza Dog** from Tomorrowland Terrace to fuel up for the morning.

Midday: Explore the Classics

- **Peter Pan's Flight**: Head to Fantasyland to soar over Neverland on this enchanting ride.

- **It's a Small World**: Enjoy a calming boat ride filled with cheerful music and colorful displays.

- **Lunch Break**: Dine at **Hungry Bear Restaurant** in Westernland for hearty Japanese curry. Pro tip: Sit near the river for a peaceful view.

Afternoon: Dive into Adventure

- **Pirates of the Caribbean**: Set sail on a swashbuckling adventure in Adventureland.

- **Splash Mountain**: Cool off with a thrilling drop into Critter Country.

- **Take a Breather**: Stroll along the Westernland River Trail for some tranquility.

Evening: End with a Bang

1. **Dinner**: Enjoy a magical meal at **Queen of Hearts Banquet Hall** in Fantasyland.
2. **Catch the Parade**: Secure a spot for the **Tokyo Disneyland Electrical Parade: DreamLights**. Arrive early for the best view.
3. **Nightcap Ride**: Wrap up your day with a ride on **Big Thunder Mountain**, which feels even more exciting under the night sky.
4. **Fireworks**: Don't miss **Reach for the Stars**, a stunning fireworks display that's the perfect finale.

Three-Day Immersive Experience

For those with the luxury of time, a three-day trip allows you to dive deep into all the magic Tokyo Disneyland and DisneySea have to offer.

Day 1: Explore Tokyo Disneyland

- Follow the **One-Day Adventure Plan** but take it slower, allowing more time for shopping, exploring hidden gems, and savoring meals.
- Bonus Tip: Visit **Tom Sawyer Island** for some relaxed exploration and interactive fun.

Day 2: Dive into DisneySea

- Spend the second day at **Tokyo DisneySea**, the park's ocean-themed sibling. Must-dos include:
  - **Journey to the Center of the Earth**: A thrilling ride that combines storytelling and speed.
  - **Soaring: Fantastic Flight**: A breathtaking flight simulator with stunning visuals.
  - **Dining**: Have lunch at **Magellan's**, a fine-dining restaurant housed in a Renaissance-style fortress.

Day 3: Revisit Favorites and Indulge

- Return to Tokyo Disneyland to revisit your favorite attractions or catch anything you missed.

- Focus on entertainment like **Mickey's Magical Music World** at Fantasyland Forest Theatre.
- Spend time shopping for souvenirs and enjoying seasonal treats.

Thematic Itineraries

These itineraries cater to specific travel styles, ensuring you make the most of your day no matter what you're looking for.

Family-Friendly Fun

This itinerary is designed for families with kids, focusing on gentle rides, character interactions, and plenty of rest stops.

Morning: Start with Magic

- **Meet Mickey Mouse**: Begin your day in Toontown with a visit to Mickey's House. The photo op with Mickey is a must for little ones.
- **It's a Small World**: Head to Fantasyland for a colorful, music-filled boat ride that's perfect for kids.
- **Morning Snack**: Grab **Alien Mochi** in Tomorrowland to keep everyone energized.

Midday: Take It Easy

- **Pooh's Hunny Hunt**: A trackless ride through the Hundred Acre Wood that's as whimsical as it is fun.

- **Lunch**: Stop by **Grandma Sara's Kitchen** for comforting Japanese meals in a cozy, kid-friendly setting.

Afternoon: Fun and Games

- **Buzz Lightyear's Astro Blasters**: A kid-friendly, interactive ride in Tomorrowland.

- **Parade Time**: Catch the daytime parade, **Disney Harmony in Color**, for a magical experience.

- **Rest Break**: Visit the Hub Gardens for a quiet moment before diving back into the action.

Evening: Wrap Up the Day

- **Dinner**: Head to **Eastside Cafe** for a simple, pasta-based meal that kids will enjoy.

- **Fireworks**: End the day with **Reach for the Stars**, marveling at the display from the Central Plaza.

Thrill-Seeker's Guide

If adrenaline is your middle name, this itinerary is all about the most heart-pounding attractions.

Morning: Kickstart the Excitement

- **Space Mountain**: Begin with a high-speed journey through the cosmos.
- **Big Thunder Mountain**: Keep the adrenaline flowing with a wild ride through the canyons of Westernland.

Midday: Adventure Awaits

- **Pirates of the Caribbean**: Embark on a thrilling pirate escapade.
- **Splash Mountain**: Cool off with an exhilarating drop into Critter Country.
- **Lunch**: Recharge at **Hungry Bear Restaurant** with a plate of curry.

Afternoon: Unleash Your Inner Explorer

- **Jungle Cruise**: A light-hearted yet adventurous ride through untamed jungles.
- **FastPass Alert**: Secure a spot for **Enchanted Tale of Beauty and the Beast** for a late-afternoon thrill.

Evening: Nighttime Adventures

- **Dinner**: Enjoy dinner at **Crystal Palace Restaurant** for a sophisticated yet satisfying meal.

- **DreamLights Parade**: Take a break and enjoy the glowing parade.

- **Nightcap Ride**: Head back to Space Mountain for an electrifying finale under the stars.

Romantic Getaway

For couples, Tokyo Disneyland offers magical moments and cozy experiences that make it a perfect destination for romance.

Morning: Start with Elegance

- **Breakfast**: Share a quiet meal at **Crystal Palace Restaurant**.

- **Cinderella Castle Walkthrough**: Begin your day with a dreamy stroll through the castle, soaking in the fairy tale atmosphere.

Midday: Cherish the Moments

- **Peter Pan's Flight**: Fly over London and Neverland together on this charming ride.

- **Lunch**: Dine at **Queen of Hearts Banquet Hall**, where the whimsical decor sets the mood.

- **Fantasyland Forest Theatre**: Catch a live performance of **Mickey's Magical Music World** for a heartfelt experience.

Afternoon: Romantic Strolls

- **Westernland River Trail**: Enjoy a scenic walk along the river, hand in hand.

- **Tom Sawyer Island**: Escape the crowds and explore this quiet, interactive retreat.

Evening: Magical Finale

- **Dinner**: End your day with a candlelit meal at **Magellan's** in DisneySea or **Eastside Cafe** in Disneyland.

- **Fireworks**: Watch **Reach for the Stars** from a cozy spot near the castle for a perfect ending.

Bonus Tips for All Itineraries:

- **Use the App**: The Tokyo Disneyland app helps you track wait times, make reservations, and find your way around the park.

- **Hydrate and Rest**: Don't forget to stay hydrated and take breaks there are plenty of shaded areas and cozy spots to relax.

- **Capture the Memories**: Take plenty of photos, but don't forget to put the camera down and soak in the magic around you.

Tokyo Disneyland has something for every kind of traveler, and with these itineraries, you're set to make the most of your visit.

Transportation and Navigation

Navigating Tokyo Disneyland and its surrounding areas can be a seamless experience with the right information. Let's delve into the essentials to ensure your visit is both enjoyable and stress-free.

Getting Around the Park

Tokyo Disneyland is designed for easy navigation, with clearly marked pathways and ample signage in both Japanese and English. Here's how to make the most of your movement within the park:

1. Park Maps

- **Physical Maps**: Available at the entrance, these maps provide a comprehensive overview of attractions, dining, and facilities.
- **Digital Maps**: Accessible via the official Tokyo Disney Resort App, offering real-time updates and GPS functionality.

2. Signage

- **Bilingual Signs**: Throughout the park, signs are in Japanese and English, guiding you to attractions, restrooms, and dining areas.

3. **Accessibility**

- **Stroller and Wheelchair Rentals**: Available near the entrance for a nominal fee, ensuring comfort for all guests.

- **Accessible Routes**: The park is equipped with ramps and designated viewing areas for guests with mobility needs.

4. **Cast Members**

- **Assistance**: Friendly staff, known as Cast Members, are stationed throughout the park to assist with directions and information.

Pro Tip: Familiarize yourself with the park layout before your visit using the official website or app to plan your day efficiently.

Using the Disney Resort Line

The Disney Resort Line is a monorail system that encircles Tokyo Disney Resort, connecting key destinations.

1. **Overview**

- **Stations**: The line includes four stations:

- **Resort Gateway Station**: Near Maihama Station, serving as the main entrance to the resort.

- **Tokyo Disneyland Station**: Direct access to Tokyo Disneyland.

- **Bayside Station**: Access to official hotels and the Disney Ambassador Hotel.

- **Tokyo DisneySea Station**: Direct access to Tokyo DisneySea.

2. Tickets and Fares

- **Ticket Purchase**: Tickets can be bought at automated machines or counters at each station.

- **Fares**: A single ride costs ¥260.

- **Day Passes**: Unlimited rides are available with day passes:
    - **1-Day Pass**: ¥660
    - **2-Day Pass**: ¥850
    - **3-Day Pass**: ¥1,200
    - **4-Day Pass**: ¥1,500

3. Operating Hours

- **Schedule**: The monorail operates from 6:00 AM to 12:05 AM, with trains arriving every 4-13 minutes.

Pro Tip: Keep your ticket handy, as you'll need it to enter and exit the stations.

Navigating Tokyo Disney Resort with Apps and Maps

Leveraging technology can enhance your experience and streamline navigation.

1. Official Tokyo Disney Resort App

- **Features**:
    - **Real-Time Wait Times**: Stay updated on attraction queues.
    - **Show Schedules**: Plan your day around entertainment offerings.
    - **Restaurant Reservations**: Secure dining spots in advance.
    - **Digital Maps**: Navigate the park with ease.
- **Availability**: Free to download on iOS and Android devices.

2. Google Maps

- **Usage**: Provides detailed directions within the resort and surrounding areas.

Pro Tip: Ensure your smartphone is charged, and consider carrying a portable charger to stay connected throughout the day.

Parking and Shuttle Services

For guests arriving by car or staying at nearby hotels, understanding parking and shuttle options is crucial.

1. Parking

- **Locations**:
    - **Tokyo Disneyland Parking**: Adjacent to the park entrance.
    - **Tokyo DisneySea Parking**: Near the DisneySea entrance.
- **Fees**:
    - **Standard Vehicles**: ¥2,500 on weekdays; ¥3,000 on weekends and holidays.
    - **Oversized Vehicles**: ¥4,500.

- **Operating Hours**: Parking lots open 1 hour before park opening and close 1 hour after park closing.

2. Shuttle Services

- **Disney Resort Cruiser**: Complimentary buses connecting official hotels with the parks and Ikspiari shopping complex.
- **Hotel Shuttles**: Many partner hotels offer free shuttle services to and from the resort.

Pro Tip: If staying at a partner hotel, inquire about shuttle schedules upon check-in to coordinate your travel plans.

By familiarizing yourself with these transportation and navigation options, you can focus on creating magical memories without the stress of logistics. Enjoy your adventure at Tokyo Disneyland!

Safety and Health Tips

Safety and well-being are essential parts of creating magical memories. With over 20 years of exploring every corner of Tokyo Disneyland, I've experienced it all from crowded parades to sudden weather changes. Here's your comprehensive guide to staying safe and healthy, tailored to ensure your visit is worry-free and full of joy.

Staying Safe in Crowded Areas

Tokyo Disneyland attracts millions of visitors annually, and navigating through bustling spaces can be part of the experience. With a few mindful practices, you can stay safe and enjoy the magic.

1. Plan Your Arrival and Departure

- **Arrive Early**: Beat the rush by entering the park as it opens, typically at 8:00 AM. This gives you a head start on popular attractions.

- **Avoid Peak Times**: If possible, plan your visit on weekdays and avoid national holidays or school vacation periods like Golden Week in late April.

2. Navigate the Crowds

- **Stick to the Edges**: When moving through crowded areas like World Bazaar or during parades, walk along the edges of pathways to avoid congestion.

- **Set Meeting Points**: Establish a central spot (like the Partners Statue near Cinderella Castle) where your group can reunite if separated.

3. Mind Your Belongings

- **Use Secure Bags**: Choose a crossbody or zippered backpack to keep valuables safe. Consider using small locks for added security.

- **Avoid Flashy Accessories**: Keep expensive items subtle to avoid unnecessary attention.

Pro Tip: If the crowds feel overwhelming, retreat to quieter areas like the Hub Gardens or Tom Sawyer Island for a break.

Preparing for Weather Changes

Japan's weather can shift dramatically, and Tokyo Disneyland is no exception. Being prepared ensures you're comfortable and ready for anything.

1. Understand the Seasons

- **Spring (March to May)**: Mild and pleasant, but rain showers are common. Carry a compact umbrella or rain poncho.

- **Summer (June to August)**: Hot and humid, with temperatures often exceeding 30°C (86°F). Wear breathable clothing and bring sunscreen.

- **Autumn (September to November)**: Cooler temperatures, but typhoon season may bring occasional storms.

- **Winter (December to February)**: Chilly, especially in the evenings. Layer up with a warm jacket and scarf.

2. Pack Smart

- **Essentials**:
    - Lightweight raincoat or poncho (available at park shops).

- Refillable water bottle to stay hydrated.
- Travel-size sunscreen and lip balm with SPF.
- A small, portable fan for summer visits.

3. Take Shelter When Needed

- **Indoor Attractions**: Escape sudden downpours or intense heat by visiting covered rides like *Pirates of the Caribbean* or *Enchanted Tale of Beauty and the Beast*.
- **Restaurants and Cafes**: Use meal breaks to avoid bad weather while refueling.

Pro Tip: Check weather forecasts regularly through apps like Japan Weather or the Tokyo Disney Resort app for real-time updates.

First Aid Stations and Emergency Services

No one plans for accidents or health issues, but knowing where to find help can provide peace of mind.

1. **First Aid Stations**

   - **Location**: The main First Aid Station is near World Bazaar, close to the park entrance.

   - **Services**:
     - Basic medical assistance for minor injuries or illnesses.
     - Supplies such as band-aids, antiseptics, and cold packs.

   Pro Tip: If you or a loved one has a specific medical condition, carry a translated note explaining your needs in Japanese to help staff assist you efficiently.

2. **Emergency Assistance**

   - **Cast Members Are Trained**: Every Cast Member knows how to handle emergencies. Don't hesitate to ask for help if needed.

   - **On-Site Medical Team**: In severe cases, the park has protocols to connect guests with local hospitals.

3. **Prepare for Your Day**

   - **Pack Medication**: Bring any prescription drugs you need, as pharmacies nearby may not stock specific items.

- **Allergies**: If you have food allergies, notify restaurant staff. Allergy cards in Japanese can be helpful.

COVID-19 Precautions and Updates

Tokyo Disneyland has adjusted its operations to prioritize guest safety during the ongoing COVID-19 situation.

1. Hygiene Measures

- **Hand Sanitizer Stations**: Located throughout the park, especially at attraction entrances and dining areas.
- **Enhanced Cleaning**: High-touch surfaces like ride restraints and railings are sanitized regularly.

2. Mask Guidelines

- **Recommended**: Masks are encouraged indoors and in crowded outdoor spaces. Many guests follow this practice for added safety.
- **Bring Extras**: Pack a few masks in case they get damp or uncomfortable.

3. Health Monitoring

- **Temperature Checks**: Conducted at park entrances. Guests with a fever or symptoms may be denied entry.
- **Stay Home if Unwell**: If you're feeling under the weather, it's better to postpone your visit.

Pro Tip: Stay updated on Tokyo Disneyland's latest health and safety policies through their official website or app.

Additional Safety Tips for Families

- **Child Safety Measures**:
    - Use wristbands or ID tags with your contact information for young children.
    - Strollers are available for rent at the park entrance.
- **Lost and Found**:
    - Report lost items to Guest Services near the park entrance or use the app to file a claim.
- **Emergency Contacts**:
    - Keep local emergency numbers handy:

- **Police**: 110
- **Ambulance/Fire**: 119
- **Tokyo Disney Guest Hotline**: +81-45-330-5211

When safety becomes second nature, you can focus on what truly matters creating magical memories. Whether it's staying hydrated, preparing for sudden rain, or navigating crowds, a little foresight goes a long way. With these tips, you'll be ready to enjoy every moment of your Tokyo Disneyland adventure with confidence and peace of mind.

Packing and Preparation Tips

Preparing for your trip to Tokyo Disneyland can make the difference between a smooth, magical day and a stressful one. I've learned a thing or two about how to pack smartly and plan wisely. Here's your ultimate checklist, tailored to every traveler's needs.

What to Pack for Your Disney Adventure

Packing for Tokyo Disneyland isn't just about essentials it's about setting yourself up for a day filled with comfort and fun. Here's what you'll need:

1. Clothing and Comfort

- **Weather-Appropriate Attire**:
    - Spring/Fall: Layered clothing for cool mornings and warmer afternoons.
    - Summer: Lightweight, breathable clothes; bring a hat or cap to shield yourself from the sun.

- Winter: Warm jackets, gloves, and scarves Tokyo can get surprisingly cold.

- **Comfortable Shoes**:
    - Expect to walk a lot. Choose supportive sneakers or well-cushioned walking shoes.
    - Avoid brand-new shoes; break them in beforehand.

2. Weather Protection

- **Rain Gear**:
    - Compact umbrella or rain poncho (you can buy themed ponchos in the park if needed).
    - Waterproof bags or pouches to protect electronics.

- **Sun Protection**:
    - Sunscreen with high SPF.
    - Sunglasses with UV protection.
    - Reusable water bottle to stay hydrated.

3. Park Essentials

- **Tickets and Passes**:

- - Print your tickets or save them on your phone (via the Tokyo Disney Resort app).
  - Bring ID if required for special passes or promotions.
- **Backpack or Tote**:
  - Choose a lightweight, secure bag to carry your belongings.
- **Portable Charger**:
  - Keep your phone charged for photos, navigation, and app usage.

4. **Snacks and Water**
   - **Snacks**:
     - Pack a few portable, non-messy snacks like granola bars, crackers, or nuts.
     - While the park offers amazing food options, having backups is always a good idea.
   - **Water Bottle**:
     - There are water fountains throughout the park where you can refill.

Essential Gear for Families with Kids

Traveling with children? Packing thoughtfully can make your day much smoother. Here's a checklist designed specifically for families:

1. Baby and Toddler Must-Haves

- **Stroller**:
  - Bring your own or rent one near the park entrance. Rentals are sturdy and convenient.

- **Diaper Bag**:
  - Stock it with diapers, wipes, a changing mat, and plastic bags for disposal.

- **Baby Food and Bottles**:
  - Pre-pack meals and formula for babies; warming stations are available at Baby Care Centers.

- **Favorite Toys/Blanket**:
  - Comfort items can help calm little ones during long waits or nap times.

2. Older Kids' Needs

- **Activity Kit**:
    - Coloring books, small toys, or travel games to keep them entertained during downtime.
- **Snacks and Drinks**:
    - Easy-to-carry, kid-friendly snacks and a reusable water bottle.
- **Rain Gear**:
    - Kid-sized ponchos or umbrellas in case of sudden rain.

3. Emergency Kit

- **First Aid Basics**:
    - Band-aids, antiseptic wipes, fever reducers, and anti-itch cream.
- **Extra Clothes**:
    - Pack a spare set of clothes for each child, especially if they plan to enjoy water rides or messy treats.

Pro Tip: Label your child's belongings with your contact information. In crowded areas, a simple ID bracelet or tag can be incredibly helpful.

Recommended Apps and Tools

Technology can be your best ally at Tokyo Disneyland. These apps and tools will simplify your visit and help you make the most of your time.

1. Tokyo Disney Resort App

This official app is a must-have for navigating the park.

- **Features**:
    - View real-time wait times for rides.
    - Book dining reservations and purchase Premier Access (FastPass replacement).
    - Check showtimes and event schedules.
- **Download**: Available for both iOS and Android. Ensure it's set up before your visit.

Pro Tip: Enable location services for personalized recommendations and navigation within the park.

2. Translation Apps

While many signs and instructions are in English, a translation app can be handy for menus or less common scenarios.

- **Google Translate**: Offers camera translation for menus and signs.
- **Papago**: Another excellent option with a user-friendly interface.

3. Weather Apps

Keep an eye on the forecast to prepare for sudden changes.

- **Japan Weather**: Tailored to Japan, with accurate forecasts and alerts.
- **AccuWeather**: Offers real-time updates for the park's location.

Pro Tip: Bookmark the Tokyo Disney Resort website on your phone for quick access to updates and guidelines.

4. Navigation Tools

Getting to the park and moving around Tokyo can be daunting without the right tools.

- **Google Maps**: Essential for planning your route to the park.
- **Japan Travel by NAVITIME**: Great for navigating Japan's public transportation system.

Additional Tips for a Smooth Trip

- **Practice Packing**: Test your bag setup before the trip to ensure it's not too heavy or cumbersome.

- **Use Ziplock Bags**: Organize small items like snacks, electronics, or first aid supplies in labeled bags.

- **Cash and Cards**: While most places accept credit cards, having some yen on hand is helpful for small purchases or emergencies.

- **Plan for Souvenirs**: Leave space in your bag for Disney merchandise or consider bringing a foldable tote.

Quick Checklist for Every Traveler

Must-Have Essentials

- Tickets and IDs
- Comfortable shoes
- Weather-appropriate clothing
- Sunscreen and sunglasses
- Water bottle

For Families

- Stroller and diaper bag
- Toys and activity kits

- Spare clothes

Tech and Tools

- Portable charger
- Tokyo Disney Resort app
- Translation and navigation apps

Extras

- First aid supplies
- Snacks
- Lightweight rain gear

Packing and preparation don't have to be overwhelming. With this checklist and a little planning, you'll be ready to explore the magic of Tokyo Disneyland with confidence and ease.

Insider Tips and Tricks

If you're planning your Tokyo Disneyland adventure, let me play the role of your savvy, well-traveled friend who knows every trick in the book. I've picked up insider knowledge that will save you time, money, and maybe even a little stress. Let's make sure your trip is as magical as it is efficient!

How to Avoid Long Lines

Lines are inevitable at any Disney Park, but there are plenty of clever ways to dodge the longest waits. Here's how to work smarter, not harder.

1. Arrive Early

- **Why It Works**: The park officially opens at 8:00 AM, but guests can queue up before that. Arriving 30–60 minutes early lets you be among the first to enter, giving you a head start on popular attractions.

- **Pro Tip**: Head straight to *Enchanted Tale of Beauty and the Beast* or *Space Mountain*. These rides tend to attract the biggest crowds.

2. Use Premier Access (FastPass Replacement)

- **What It Is**: Premier Access is a paid system that allows you to book a designated time for select attractions via the Tokyo Disney Resort App.

- **How to Use It**: As soon as you enter the park, open the app and book your Premier Access for high-demand rides like *Splash Mountain* or *Big Thunder Mountain*.

- **Pro Tip**: Book Premier Access for your top-priority ride first, then hit less crowded attractions while you wait.

3. Timing Is Everything

- **During Parades**: Lines for rides tend to drop during parades and nighttime shows like *DreamLights* and *Reach for the Stars*. Use this time to hit popular attractions.

- **Meal Times**: Between 12:00 PM and 2:00 PM, many guests are dining. Take advantage of this lull to tackle high-demand rides.

Best Times to Visit Popular Attractions

Timing is key when it comes to making the most of your day. Here's a guide to the best times for some of the park's must-see spots.

1. Morning: Hit the Big Ones

- **First Hour Focus**:
    - *Space Mountain*: One of the fastest to build a line. Ride this early or book Premier Access.
    - *Pooh's Hunny Hunt*: Unique to Tokyo Disneyland and wildly popular head here first if you love whimsical adventures.

2. Afternoon: Opt for Lower Wait Times

- **Hidden Gems**:
    - *Jungle Cruise*: Less crowded after lunchtime.
    - *It's a Small World*: A calm, air-conditioned ride that rarely has long waits.

3. **Evening: Ride Under the Stars**

- **Thrilling Night Rides**:
    - *Big Thunder Mountain*: Feels more intense and magical at night.
    - *Splash Mountain*: The illuminated views of Critter Country add a special touch.

Pro Tip: The last hour before park closing often sees the shortest lines. Save a top-priority ride for this time if you can stay late.

Where to Find the Best Photo Spots

Tokyo Disneyland is a photographer's dream. From iconic backdrops to hidden gems, here are the best places to snap unforgettable pictures.

1. Cinderella Castle

- **Classic View**: The Central Plaza offers the perfect head-on shot of the castle.
- **Unique Angles**: Walk to the bridge connecting Fantasyland and Westernland for a quieter, side-profile shot.
- **Pro Tip**: Visit at golden hour (around sunset) for soft, dreamy lighting.

2. Toontown

- **Quirky Details**: From Mickey's House to Roger Rabbit's Car Toon Spin, this area is full of vibrant, playful photo ops.

- **Pro Tip**: Use Toontown's interactive props (like oversized doors and zany fountains) for fun, creative shots.

3. World Bazaar

- **Rainy Day Charm**: The glass-covered streets create a cozy atmosphere for photos even during bad weather.

- **Seasonal Displays**: Check out the ever-changing seasonal decorations for unique backdrops.

4. Critter Country

- **Rustic Vibes**: The riverbank near Splash Mountain is picturesque and often less crowded.

- **Pro Tip**: Capture the log flume splash for a dynamic action shot.

Pro Tip: Always have your phone or camera-ready parades, characters, and surprise performances can create spontaneous photo moments.

Budget-Saving Hacks

A visit to Tokyo Disneyland doesn't have to break the bank. Here are some clever ways to save without sacrificing the experience.

1. Bring Your Own Snacks and Drinks

- **Why It Saves**: While the park has amazing food, bringing snacks can help cut costs and keep you energized between meals.
- **What to Pack**: Granola bars, fruit, and a reusable water bottle (there are refill stations throughout the park).

2. Buy Tickets in Advance

- **How It Helps**: Purchasing your tickets online before your trip not only saves time but also ensures you get the best rate.
- **Pro Tip**: Consider bundled tickets if you're visiting both Tokyo Disneyland and DisneySea.

3. Shop Strategically

- **Pre-Budget Your Souvenirs**: Decide in advance how much you'll spend on merchandise.

- **Buy Multipurpose Items**: Look for items that can be used at home, like mugs, bento boxes, or kitchenware.

4. Stay Offsite

- **Affordable Hotels Nearby**: If official Disney hotels are out of budget, there are plenty of nearby options with shuttle services to the park.
- **Pro Tip**: Book early for the best deals, especially during peak seasons.

Bonus Tips for the Ultimate Experience

1. Use the Tokyo Disney Resort App

- Track wait times, reserve dining, and navigate the park with ease. It's your best friend for planning on the go.

2. Take Advantage of Single Rider Lines

- Available on select attractions, these lines are usually much shorter and perfect if you're willing to ride solo.

3. Stay for the Fireworks

- Even if you've had a long day, stick around for *Reach for the Stars*. The view from the Central Plaza is breathtaking.

4. Pack Smart

- Bring a portable charger, rain gear, and a lightweight bag to keep your essentials handy without weighing you down.

By following these tips and tricks, you'll feel like a Tokyo Disneyland pro, gliding past long lines, capturing stunning photos, and making magical memories without stretching your budget. So go ahead embrace the magic with confidence and style!

Sustainability and Responsible Tourism

As travelers, our adventures shape the world we visit, and Tokyo Disneyland is no exception. By embracing sustainability and responsible tourism, we can ensure that the magic we experience today remains vibrant for generations to come. Let me guide you through the eco-friendly practices at Tokyo Disneyland and how you, as a visitor, can play an essential role in preserving its beauty while respecting the culture and environment of Japan.

Eco-Friendly Practices at Tokyo Disneyland

Tokyo Disneyland is more than just a theme park; it's a model of innovation and commitment to sustainability. Here are the ways the park is working to minimize its environmental impact:

1. Waste Management and Recycling

- **Recycling Stations**: Strategically placed throughout the park, these stations allow guests to separate their waste into recyclables and non-recyclables. You'll often see clearly labeled bins for plastic bottles, paper, and general waste.

- **Reusable Items**: Restaurants and food stalls have transitioned to using washable plates, cutlery, and cups in many locations, reducing single-use plastics.

Fun Fact: Disney has been a leader in waste reduction for decades, with Tokyo Disneyland continuously improving its recycling rates.

2. Energy Efficiency

- **LED Lighting**: Most of the park's lighting has been upgraded to energy-efficient LED systems, including the iconic Cinderella Castle, which glows with sustainable brilliance every evening.

- **Green Power**: Tokyo Disneyland incorporates renewable energy sources, such as solar panels, to power parts of the resort.

Did You Know? Even the park's electric vehicles, like the monorail and service carts, are designed with energy efficiency in mind.

3. Sustainable Food Practices

- **Locally Sourced Ingredients**: Many of the park's restaurants prioritize using seasonal and locally sourced ingredients, reducing the carbon footprint of their meals.

- **Food Waste Reduction**: Leftover food from restaurants is repurposed or composted wherever possible, turning waste into valuable resources.

4. Water Conservation

- **Advanced Irrigation**: Gardens and green spaces are maintained using efficient irrigation systems that minimize water waste.

- **Water Recycling**: Attractions that use water, such as the Rivers of America and Splash Mountain, rely on sophisticated systems to recycle and clean water continuously.

How Visitors Can Support Sustainability

Your actions as a visitor can significantly contribute to Tokyo Disneyland's sustainability efforts. Here are some simple but impactful steps you can take:

1. **Reduce Waste**

   - **Bring a Reusable Water Bottle**: There are water fountains and refill stations throughout the park. This eliminates the need for single-use plastic bottles.

   - **Carry a Reusable Bag**: Use a foldable shopping bag for any souvenirs you purchase, as Japan encourages reducing plastic waste.

2. **Choose Eco-Friendly Transportation**

   - **Public Transit**: The most sustainable way to reach Tokyo Disneyland is by train. The JR Keiyo Line takes you directly to Maihama Station, just a short walk from the park entrance.

   - **Disney Resort Line**: Once at the resort, use the monorail to get around its electric and highly efficient.

Pro Tip: Walking between nearby hotels and park entrances is a great way to reduce energy consumption while staying active.

3. **Be Mindful of Food Choices**

   - **Order Wisely**: Only order what you can finish to help minimize food waste. Portions at Tokyo Disneyland are often generous, so sharing is a great idea.

- **Support Sustainable Dining**: Seek out restaurants that highlight locally sourced and seasonal ingredients. Not only is the food fresher, but it also supports local farmers.

4. Use the Tokyo Disney Resort App Wisely

- **Digital Tickets**: opt for e-tickets to reduce paper waste. The app allows you to store tickets and Premier Access passes digitally.

- **Plan Efficiently**: Use the app to monitor wait times and schedules, minimizing unnecessary walking and conserving energy.

5. Pack Sustainably

- **Eco-Friendly Essentials**: Pack items like bamboo utensils, silicone straws, and reusable snack containers to cut down on disposable waste.

- **Travel Light**: A lighter suitcase means less fuel consumption during travel every little bit counts!

Respecting Local Culture and Environment

Tokyo Disneyland is a magical blend of global Disney charm and rich Japanese traditions.

Respecting the culture and environment of Japan not only enhances your experience but also shows gratitude to the community hosting your adventure.

1. Follow the Rules

- **No Littering**: Japan takes pride in its cleanliness, and Tokyo Disneyland is no exception. Use the designated bins and avoid leaving waste behind.
- **Stay on Paths**: Whether you're exploring the gardens or walking through attractions, stick to marked paths to protect the landscape.

2. Respect Japanese Etiquette

- **Queueing**: Waiting in orderly lines is a hallmark of Japanese culture. Respect the queuing process, even during parades or for rides.
- **Politeness**: A simple "arigato" (thank you) goes a long way. Show appreciation to Cast Members for their incredible hospitality.

3. Engage with Local Traditions

- **Seasonal Events**: Tokyo Disneyland incorporates Japanese holidays into its events, such as *Oshogatsu* (New Year's) and cherry blossom season. Participate in these celebrations to connect with the culture.

- **Japanese Cuisine**: Try traditional dishes like bento boxes or mochi to experience authentic flavors.

Pro Tip: Check out the park's unique merchandise inspired by Japanese design these make excellent souvenirs and support local creativity.

Why Sustainability Matters

Every small effort we make contributes to the longevity of the places we love. By traveling responsibly and practicing sustainability, we ensure that Tokyo Disneyland remains a magical haven for future generations. As a guest, you have the power to make a positive impactone refillable water bottle, eco-friendly snack, or kind gesture at a time.

Quick Checklist for Sustainable Travel to Tokyo Disneyland

1. **Before Your Trip**:
    - Purchase e-tickets to save paper.
    - Pack reusable items like water bottles, bags, and utensils.
    - Plan to use public transportation.
2. **At the Park**:

- Use recycling bins for waste.
- Refill water bottles at fountains.
- Respect the environment by staying on paths and using bins.

3. **Dining and Shopping**:
    - Choose restaurants with locally sourced ingredients.
    - Buy multipurpose souvenirs that reduce waste.

4. **Engage Responsibly**:
    - Participate in seasonal events to support local culture.
    - Follow Park rules and show politeness to Cast Members and fellow visitors.

By adopting these practices, you'll not only enjoy a more fulfilling visit but also leave a positive footprint behind. Together, we can keep the magic of Tokyo Disneyland alive and thriving for all who come to experience its wonder.

Resources and Contacts

Planning a trip to Tokyo Disneyland is an exciting adventure, and having the right resources at your fingertips can make your experience seamless and enjoyable. To ensure you're well-prepared, here's a comprehensive guide to essential contacts and tools, complete with direct links and contact details.

Official Websites and Apps

Tokyo Disney Resort offers a range of official digital resources to assist you in planning and enhancing your visit.

1. Tokyo Disney Resort Official Website

The official website provides comprehensive information on attractions, events, tickets, accommodations, and more.

- **Website**: Tokyo Disney Resort Official Website

2. Tokyo Disney Resort App

This official app is a must-have for navigating the parks efficiently.

- **Features**:

- Purchase Park tickets online.
- View real-time wait times for attractions.
- Make restaurant reservations.
- Access Park maps and your current location.
- Utilize Disney Premier Access for select attractions.

- **Download**:
    - **iOS**: App Store
    - **Android**: Google Play

Note: The app is available in English and Japanese. Ensure your smartphone's language setting is set to your preferred language for optimal use.

Local Emergency Numbers

While Tokyo Disneyland is a safe and well-managed environment, it's essential to be prepared for any unexpected situations. Here are crucial emergency contact numbers in Japan:

- **Police (Emergency)**: 110
- **Fire and Ambulance**: 119

- **Japan Helpline**: 0570-000-911
    - A 24/7 service offering assistance in English for various non-emergency situations.

Tip: Program these numbers into your mobile phone before your trip for quick access if needed.

Contact Details for Tokyo Disney Resort

For any inquiries or assistance related to your visit, Tokyo Disney Resort provides several contact options:

1. Tokyo Disney Resort Information Center

- **Phone**:
    - **Within Japan**: 050-3090-2742
    - **International**: +81-50-3090-2742
- **Operating Hours**: 10:00 AM to 3:00 PM (Japan Standard Time), 7 days a week.
- **Language**: Assistance available in English.

Note: Call charges will differ based on your phone carrier and plan. Please contact your phone carrier for details.

2. Online Inquiries

For non-urgent matters or if you prefer written communication, you can use the online contact form:

- **Contact Form**: Tokyo Disney Resort Contact Form

Note: Response times may vary; for immediate assistance, calling is recommended.

3. Lost and found at Disney Hotels

If you've misplaced an item during your stay at a Disney hotel, contact the hotel directly:

- **Tokyo Disneyland Hotel**: 047-305-3333
- **Disney Ambassador Hotel**: 047-305-1111
- **Tokyo DisneySea Hotel MiraCosta**: 047-305-2222
- **Tokyo Disney Resort Toy Story Hotel**: 047-305-5555
- **Tokyo Disney Celebration Hotel**: 047-381-1188

Note: For international calls, dial Japan's country code (+81) and omit the leading zero.

Additional Tips

- **Time Zone**: Japan Standard Time (JST), UTC +9.

- **Language**: While many staff members speak English, learning a few basic Japanese phrases can enhance your experience.

- **Currency**: Japanese Yen (¥).

Tip: Currency exchange services are available at the resort, but it's advisable to have some yen on hand upon arrival.

By keeping these resources and contacts handy, you'll be well-equipped to navigate your Tokyo Disneyland adventure with confidence. Remember, preparation is key to a magical and stress-free experience.

Conclusion

As I sit here reflecting on my countless visits to Tokyo Disneyland over the years, I can't help but feel a profound sense of gratitude for the magic this place brings to life. Tokyo Disneyland isn't just a theme park it's a world of wonder, where dreams come alive in the most enchanting ways. It's a destination that captures the hearts of visitors from every corner of the globe, offering an unforgettable mix of nostalgia, cultural charm, and cutting-edge imagination.

Final Tips for a Magical Adventure

1. Plan, but Leave Room for Spontaneity

One of the best pieces of advice I can offer is to strike a balance between planning and letting the magic unfold naturally. Yes, you'll want to book Premier Access for must-see rides and plan your meals at iconic restaurants, but don't forget to leave time to explore, wander, and soak in the atmosphere. Some of my favorite memories at Tokyo Disneyland weren't planned they were moments of unexpected magic that happened when I slowed down and embraced the day.

2. Embrace the Seasons

Tokyo Disneyland transforms with every season, offering a completely different experience depending on when you visit. If you're there in spring, take in the cherry blossoms and pastel-colored decorations. Summer brings vibrant parades and water-based attractions to help you cool off. Autumn is perfect for Halloween fans, with themed treats and spooky decor, while winter offers the coziness of Christmas lights and seasonal shows. No matter when you go, lean into the seasonal offerings they're what make each visit truly special.

3. Immerse Yourself in the Details

Take your time to notice the small things that make Tokyo Disneyland so magical. Peek inside windows in World Bazaar, listen to the ambient sounds in Adventureland, and study the intricate carvings on Cinderella Castle. The park is a treasure trove of stories waiting to be discovered.

4. Use the App to Maximize Your Day

The Tokyo Disney Resort app is your best friend when it comes to navigating the park. From real-time wait times to mobile dining reservations, it helps you plan on the fly and make the most of your day. Before your trip, download the app, familiarize yourself with its features, and link your tickets for a seamless experience.

5. Prioritize What Matters Most to You

With so much to see and do, it's easy to feel overwhelmed. My advice? Make a list of your top priorities whether that's riding *Space Mountain*, meeting Mickey Mouse, or sampling as many snacks as possible and focus on those. Everything else will fall into place.

6. Bring Home More Than Souvenirs

While the merchandise at Tokyo Disneyland is undeniably tempting, some of the best things you'll take home are intangible. It's the laughter shared with loved ones, the awe you felt during the fireworks, and the pure joy of being in a place where magic feels real. Savor those moments they're the ones that will stay with you long after your trip is over.

7. Respect the Culture and Environment

Finally, remember that Tokyo Disneyland is not just a magical place it's part of a larger community and culture. Show respect for Japanese customs, like queueing politely and keeping the park clean. Use the recycling bins, follow the rules, and appreciate the effort that goes into maintaining this incredible destination.

If you're still on the fence about visiting Tokyo Disneyland, let me tell you this: it's not just a trip, it's an experience that touches your heart in ways you didn't know were possible. It's the laughter of children seeing their favorite characters for the first time, the thrill of a ride that makes you feel like a kid again, the warmth of a Cast Member who makes you feel truly special.

Tokyo Disneyland is a place where time slows down and the world feels a little brighter. It's a reminder of the magic that exists in everyday life, waiting for us to find it. Whether it's your first visit or your fiftieth, this park has a way of making you feel like anything is possible.

So, pack your bags, plan your trip, and let the magic begin. Tokyo Disneyland is waiting to welcome you, and trust me you'll never forget the adventure.

BONUS CHAPTER

50 Useful Japanese Phrases for Your Tokyo Disneyland Adventure

Knowing a few Japanese phrases can make your trip to Tokyo Disneyland smoother, more enjoyable, and more respectful. Don't worry if you're not fluent, locals and Cast Members appreciate the effort, and these simple phrases will help you navigate the park like a pro. Here's an organized list of 50 essential phrases categorized for different situations.

Basic Greetings and Polite Expressions

1. **こんにちは (Konnichiwa)** – Hello / Good afternoon
   Use this friendly greeting when meeting people.

2. **おはようございます (Ohayou gozaimasu)** – Good morning
   Start your day with this polite phrase.

3. **こんばんは (Konbanwa)** – Good evening
   A perfect way to greet someone in the evening.

4. **ありがとう (Arigatou)** – Thank you (informal)
For casual interactions, like thanking a friend.

5. **ありがとうございます (Arigatou gozaimasu)** – Thank you (formal)
Use this in shops, restaurants, or with Cast Members.

6. **すみません (Sumimasen)** – Excuse me / Sorry
Useful for getting someone's attention or apologizing.

7. **はい (Hai)** – Yes
A simple affirmative.

8. **いいえ (Iie)** – No
A polite way to decline.

9. **どういたしまして (Dou itashimashite)** – You're welcome
A great response when someone thanks you.

10. **お願いします (Onegaishimasu)** – Please
Use this to politely ask for something.

Navigating the Park

11. **これは何ですか？ (Kore wa nan desu ka?)** – What is this?

Handy for figuring out menu items or attractions.

12. **〜はどこですか？(… wa doko desu ka?)** – Where is…? Replace "…" with:
    - トイレ (Toire) – restroom
    - 出口 (Deguchi) – exit
    - レストラン (Resutoran) – restaurant

13. **どうやって行きますか？(Dou yatte ikimasu ka?)** – How do I get there? Use this when asking for directions.

14. **地図をください (Chizu o kudasai)** – Can I have a map? Request a physical map if needed.

15. **これに乗れますか？(Kore ni noremasu ka?)** – Can I ride this? Useful for clarifying ride restrictions.

At Restaurants and Cafes

16. **メニューをください (Menyuu o kudasai)** – Can I have a menu? Perfect for ordering meals.

17. おすすめは何ですか？ **(Osusume wa nan desu ka?)** – What do you recommend?
Ask for the staff's favorite dishes.

18. これをください **(Kore o kudasai)** – I'll have this.
Point to an item on the menu and say this.

19. いくらですか？ **(Ikura desu ka?)** – How much is it?
Ask about prices for food or merchandise.

20. お会計をお願いします **(Okaikei o onegaishimasu)** – The bill, please.
Use this to settle your meal.

Shopping for Souvenirs

21. これはいくらですか？ **(Kore wa ikura desu ka?)** – How much is this?
Useful for inquiring about souvenir prices.

22. これを見せてください **(Kore o misete kudasai)** – Please show me this.
Ask to see an item up close.

23. ありますか？ **(Arimasu ka?)** – Do you have...?
For example:
   o 大きいサイズ (Ooki saizu) – a larger size

- 小さいサイズ (Chiisai saizu) – a smaller size

24. 他の色がありますか？ **(Hoka no iro ga arimasu ka?)** – Do you have this in another color? Perfect for finding the perfect souvenir.

25. クレジットカードは使えますか？ **(Kurejitto kaado wa tsukaemasu ka?)** – Can I use a credit card? Confirm payment options.

Meeting Characters or Cast Members

26. 写真を撮ってもいいですか？ **(Shashin o totte mo ii desu ka?)** – Can I take a picture? Politely ask for permission to take photos.

27. 一緒に写真を撮ってもいいですか？ **(Issho ni shashin o totte mo ii desu ka?)** – Can we take a picture together? Use this with Disney characters or Cast Members.

28. サインをください **(Sain o kudasai)** – Can I have your autograph? If meeting Disney characters, this is handy.

29. 楽しかったです！ (Tanoshikatta desu!) – That was fun! Share your excitement with Cast Members.

30. ありがとう、ミッキー！ (Arigatou, Mikkii!) – Thank you, Mickey! Add the character's name to make it personal.

Emergency Situations

31. 助けてください (Tasukete kudasai) – Please help me. Use this in case of an emergency.

32. 具合が悪いです (Guai ga warui desu) – I'm not feeling well. Useful for seeking medical attention.

33. 子供を見失いました (Kodomo o miushinai mashita) – I've lost my child. Inform Cast Members immediately.

34. 道に迷いました (Michi ni mayoimashita) – I'm lost. Ask for assistance to find your way.

35. 警察を呼んでください (Keisatsu o yonde kudasai) – Please call the police. For serious emergencies.

Polite Small Talk

36. 初めてです **(Hajimete desu)** – This is my first time.
Share your excitement if it's your first visit.

37. すごいですね！**(Sugoi desu ne!)** – This is amazing!
Express your awe and enthusiasm.

38. どこから来ましたか？ **(Doko kara kimashita ka?)** – Where are you from?
Engage in friendly conversations.

39. 日本が大好きです **(Nihon ga daisuki desu)** – I love Japan.
Compliments are always appreciated.

40. また来ます **(Mata kimasu)** – I'll come again.
A great way to end your visit on a positive note.

Miscellaneous Phrases

41. 分かりません **(Wakarimasen)** – I don't understand.
If you're unsure, use this phrase.

42. **もう一度お願いします (Mou ichido onegaishimasu)** – Please say it again.
Ask someone to repeat what they said.

43. **英語を話せますか？ (Eigo o hanasemasu ka?)** – Do you speak English?
Check if the person can assist in English.

44. **はい、少し (Hai, sukoshi)** – Yes, a little.
Use this if you can understand some Japanese.

45. **トイレはどこですか？ (Toire wa doko desu ka?)** – Where is the restroom?
Always helpful to know!

46. **時間は何時ですか？ (Jikan wa nanji desu ka?)** – What time is it?
Ask for the current time.

47. **待ち時間はどれくらいですか？ (Machi jikan wa dore kurai desu ka?)** – How long is the wait?
Inquire about ride or show wait times.

48. **荷物を預けられますか？ (Nimotsu o azukeraremasu ka?)** – Can I store my luggage?
For locker or storage facilities.

49. 静かにしてください **(Shizuka ni shite kudasai)** – Please be quiet. Useful in quiet zones or during shows.

50. 楽しい一日を！ **(Tanoshii ichinichi o!)** – Have a great day! Spread positivity as you enjoy your trip.

Final Tips

- **Pronunciation**: Don't worry about being perfect, Japanese speakers will appreciate your effort.

- **Body Language**: Pair phrases with gestures to make yourself understood.

- **Practice Beforehand**: Try using apps like Duolingo or Google Translate to familiarize yourself with these phrases.

By learning just, a handful of these expressions, you'll feel more confident navigating Tokyo Disneyland while also connecting with the local culture. Happy exploring!

FAQs

When planning a trip to Tokyo Disneyland, it's natural to have questions. Over the years, I've heard just about every concern from fellow travelers, and I'm here to help you feel completely prepared and confident. Let's explore the most common questions visitors ask and give you clear, straightforward answers.

General Information

1. What is Tokyo Disneyland?

Tokyo Disneyland is one of two theme parks at Tokyo Disney Resort, located in Urayasu, Chiba, near Tokyo. It opened in 1983 and is modeled after Disneyland in California, offering classic attractions, parades, shows, and that signature Disney magic.

2. Where is Tokyo Disneyland, and how do I get there?

Tokyo Disneyland is in Urayasu, just outside central Tokyo. The easiest way to get there is by train:

- Take the JR Keiyo Line or JR Musashino Line to **Maihama Station**. From there, it's a short walk to the park.

- If you're staying at a Disney or nearby hotel, many offer shuttle buses to the park.

3. What are the park hours?

Typically, Tokyo Disneyland opens at 8:00 AM and closes at 9:00 PM, but hours can vary depending on the season or special events. Always check the official website or the Tokyo Disney Resort app for the latest schedule.

Tickets and Reservations

4. How do I buy tickets?

You can purchase tickets:

- **Online**: The easiest way is through the Tokyo Disney Resort official website.

- **On the App**: Download the Tokyo Disney Resort app to buy e-tickets.

- **At the Park**: Limited on-site tickets are available, but they can sell out, especially during peak times.

Pro Tip: Buy your tickets as early as possible, especially if you're visiting during holidays or weekends.

5. Can I cancel or change my ticket?

Tickets are non-refundable, but in some cases, you can change the date or upgrade your ticket for an additional fee. Check the specific terms when purchasing your tickets online.

6. Do I need reservations for rides or restaurants?

Reservations aren't required for most attractions, but they're highly recommended for:

- **Premier Access** rides like *Enchanted Tale of Beauty and the Beast* (available through the app for an additional fee).
- **Table-Service Restaurants** like the Crystal Palace or Queen of Hearts Banquet Hall. Book these through the app or website.

Park Navigation

7. Is there an app for Tokyo Disneyland?

Yes! The **Tokyo Disney Resort App** is your best friend for navigating the park. It lets you:

- Check wait times.
- Reserve dining.
- Purchase Premier Access for rides.
- Find maps and schedules.

Download it before your visit and link your tickets for a seamless experience.

8. What's the best way to get around Tokyo Disneyland?

The park is designed for walking, and most attractions are within a 10-minute stroll of each other. If you're visiting both Tokyo Disneyland and Tokyo DisneySea, the **Disney Resort Line monorail** connects the parks and hotels.

Attractions and Entertainment

9. What are the must-see attractions?

For first-time visitors, don't miss:

- **Enchanted Tale of Beauty and the Beast**: A cutting-edge, immersive experience.

- **Pooh's Hunny Hunt**: A whimsical, trackless ride unique to Tokyo Disneyland.

- **Space Mountain**: A thrilling indoor roller coaster.

- **Pirates of the Caribbean**: A timeless Disney classic.

- **DreamLights Parade**: A nighttime spectacle of lights and music.

10. Are there height or age restrictions for rides?

Yes, some attractions have height requirements for safety. For example:

- *Space Mountain*: Minimum height of 102 cm (40 inches).
- *Big Thunder Mountain*: Minimum height of 102 cm (40 inches).

Check the park's website or ask Cast Members for details.

Dining and Snacks

11. What are the must-try foods?

Tokyo Disneyland is famous for its unique food offerings. Don't miss:

- **Mickey-shaped churros**.
- **Alien mochi**: Green mochi filled with custard, chocolate, or strawberry cream.
- **Gyoza dog**: A steamed bun with savory fillings.
- **Seasonal treats**: Look out for limited-time snacks themed to holidays or events.

12. Can I bring my own food and drinks?

Outside food is not allowed in the park, but exceptions are made for baby food or special dietary needs. There are plenty of dining options to suit all tastes and budgets.

13. Do restaurants accommodate dietary restrictions?

Yes, many restaurants can accommodate dietary needs such as vegetarian, vegan, or gluten-free options. Notify the staff at table-service restaurants, or look for allergen-friendly icons on menus.

Families and Kids

14. Is Tokyo Disneyland stroller-friendly?

Absolutely! Stroller rentals are available near the park entrance for ¥1,000 per day. The park also has plenty of stroller parking areas near attractions.

15. Are there facilities for babies and toddlers?

Yes, Baby Care Centers are located in the park and offer:

- Nursing rooms.
- Diaper-changing stations.

- Bottle-warming services.

Shopping and Souvenirs

16. What's unique about Tokyo Disneyland merchandise?

You'll find exclusive items like:

- **Themed popcorn buckets**.
- **Disney-inspired yukatas and kimonos**.
- **Seasonal plush toys and accessories**.

17. Can I shop online for Tokyo Disneyland merchandise?

Unfortunately, Tokyo Disneyland merchandise is only available in the park, so make a shopping list and grab your favorites while you're there!

Weather and Seasons

18. What's the best time of year to visit?

Each season offers something special:

- **Spring**: Cherry blossom-themed decorations and mild weather.
- **Summer**: Vibrant parades and water attractions.

- **Autumn**: Halloween celebrations with themed snacks and decor.
- **Winter**: Magical Christmas lights and cozy treats.

19. What should I pack for the weather?

- **Summer**: Lightweight clothing, sunscreen, and a hat.
- **Winter**: Warm layers, gloves, and a scarf.
- **Rainy Days**: A compact umbrella or rain poncho (also sold in the park).

Health and Safety

20. Are there first aid services in the park?

Yes, First Aid Stations are located near World Bazaar. Trained medical staff are available to assist with minor injuries or illnesses.

21. What COVID-19 precautions are in place?

Tokyo Disneyland has implemented:

- Enhanced cleaning protocols.
- Hand sanitizer stations throughout the park.
- Mask recommendations for indoor areas.

Check the latest updates on the official website.

Final Questions

22. Can I visit both parks in one day?

Yes, with a **Park Hopper ticket**, you can access both Tokyo Disneyland and Tokyo DisneySea. However, each park has so much to offer that dedicating a full day to each is recommended.

23. How do I get help if I lose something?

Visit the **Lost and Found** counter near the park entrance or speak with any Cast Member. Items are often turned in quickly.

24. Is Tokyo Disneyland worth visiting if I don't speak Japanese?

Absolutely! Many attractions have English signage, and the experience transcends language barriers. Plus, Cast Members are trained to assist international guests.

With these FAQs in hand, you're ready to embark on a magical journey to Tokyo Disneyland. Whether it's your first visit or your tenth, this incredible park is sure to leave you with memories that last a lifetime. Safe travels and have an unforgettable adventure!

Made in the USA
Las Vegas, NV
29 June 2025

24213777R00098